MW01443258

The Leader's Playbook

Mastering the Art of Leadership.
Unleashing Your True Potential.

Don K. Adams

Copyright © 2024 by Don Adams

All rights reserved.

No part of this publication may be reproduced, stored in a retrieval system, or transmitted, in any form or by any means, electronic, mechanical, photocopying, recording, or otherwise, without written permission from the authors.

Content

Transition to Leadership 16

Communication 28

Leader's Tools 54

Emotions 91

Employees 132

Inspirations 149

Epilogue 167

Introduction

Over the course of the past three decades, my professional journey has been centered on honing my skills and expertise in management. With an unwavering commitment to excellence and a relentless drive to succeed, I have dedicated countless hours and extensive firsthand experience to refine my leadership abilities. Throughout these years, I have navigated through various industries, collaborated with diverse teams, and overcome numerous challenges that have undoubtedly shaped my strategic thinking and decision-making capabilities. Drawing from this extensive managerial background, I possess an astute understanding of organizational dynamics, team-building strategies, and effective communication techniques. With each passing year spent in management roles, I continue to absorb valuable lessons which have enabled me to deliver outstanding results while fostering a positive work environment. As I reflect on my 30-year-long journey in management, it is with humility that I acknowledge the invaluable knowledge gained from both successes and failures alike - an immense asset that propels me forward on a continued path of growth and success within this dynamic field.

I have spent the last 30 years in management - from messenger supervisor, mailroom manager, office services manager, area manager, director, and executive director. What I have found throughout my career is people make you successful. You cannot do it on your own. I have received many awards, bonuses, and trips to exotic locations, all due to my success in business. Early on, I patted myself on the back and basked in my triumphant glory. As I became older, I began to realize that it was not my individual talent but the talent of those I led. We as leaders, no matter how talented, are nothing without our employees. My entire working life has been committed to customer service; I believe customer service must be in your DNA. It has to be within you. What I mean is that there are so many fake smiles and wanting to be helpful, but it's not sustainable over a long period of time. What is Customer service DNA? It's your love of helping others and treating them as if you were helping yourself. Their satisfaction is your happiness.

Bio

Don was born and raised in Brooklyn, NY. He then moved to queens and eventually ended up on Long Island.

Don's top priorities are God, family, friends, and leading and mentoring others. Don has always felt that life without these five meanings is useless. Don loves writing about leadership and how to make others a better leader. Don is also a motivation speaker and a doting Grand Pa.

You can never learn enough. From training to the human experience, I have received so much understanding through the many personalities I have encountered. I have had the pleasure of going from messenger to executive. I have attended many training sessions along with coaching sessions of my own. I have always felt this has been so helpful and necessary throughout your life. Don also holds multiple certifications across different categories.

Don has had great success and received multiple awards, starting with Messenger of the Year and all the way up to Executive of the Year.

Why I Authored This Book

I authored this book on leadership because of my experience and expertise in the field. Having spent over two decades working as a senior leader in various industries, I have witnessed firsthand the impact effective leadership can have on organizations and individuals. Throughout my career, I have honed my skills and knowledge, constantly seeking to learn from both successful and challenging experiences.

This book serves as a culmination of my insights, strategies, and principles that I believe are essential for anyone aspiring to become an exceptional leader. It is my intention to provide aspiring leaders with practical guidance and tools necessary to navigate the complexities of today's fast-paced and dynamic business world. By sharing personal anecdotes, real-life case studies, and proven frameworks, I aim to inspire readers to elevate their leadership abilities, drive meaningful change within their teams, and create a lasting impact on their organizations' success.

I authored this book to help others better understand leadership and how to become better in any leadership role. People will tell you they want to be in a leadership role; however, not everyone can thrive in this line of work. Leadership is a tough job; you must understand what your bosses think, what the client needs, and what the employee wants. There will be extremely high days and exceptionally low days. This is not a job for the easily offended or quick-tempered; you will never have success. Fortunately, there is tons of help to make you a better leader. I'm not saying there won't be low days or no pressure, but remember, no pressure, no diamonds. Remember, your success is due to your staff; therefore, you must lead. With my rich experience, I thought, why not create a playbook to help you grow your success and become the leader you were meant to be.

I embarked on years of studying and researching leadership theories, interviewing successful leaders from various fields, and analyzing their strategies to understand what sets them apart. This book is the culmination of that deep dive into leadership to share my findings with aspiring leaders like yourself. It's filled with invaluable insights, practical advice, and real-life examples that will guide you on your path to becoming a remarkable leader.

Trust me; this isn't just another run-of-the-mill self-help book—it's an honest attempt to empower individuals ready to make their mark on the world of leadership.

Manage the Process

Managing the process is a crucial aspect of any project or organizational management. It involves understanding and adhering to the established procedures, policies, and guidelines that inform the workflow, communication, and decision-making processes involved in achieving specific objectives. This approach requires effective planning, execution, monitoring, control, and evaluation of every step along the way to ensure that each task contributes optimally towards the overarching goals. Managing the process entails forethought and familiarity with best practices in project management, including resource allocation, risk identification and mitigation strategies, as well as performance measurement techniques that enable adaptation to changing circumstances with minimal disruption. It also requires clear communication channels within teams for timely coordination of efforts and efficient resolution of obstacles along the way. In implementing this approach effectively, organizations can enhance efficiencies in their operations, resulting in increased productivity while achieving higher quality outcomes within shorter timelines.

So, the reason I authored this book about leadership is simple - I believe that we could all use a little guidance when it comes to leading others. Over the years, I have had my fair share of difficulties as a leader, and through trial and error, I have learned some valuable lessons along the way. I wanted to share these lessons with others struggling or looking for inspiration in their leadership journeys.

This book is not just another theoretical guide filled with buzzwords; it is a collection of real-world stories, practical advice, and actionable tips that anyone can apply in their day-to-day lives. Leadership is not reserved for CEOs or managers; it's something we can all cultivate within ourselves, regardless of our position. By sharing my experiences and insights, I hope to empower readers with the tools they need to become influential leaders in any sphere of life.

Thank You

I just must take a moment and express my overwhelming gratitude to all the incredible individuals who have played a significant role in shaping me into the leader I am today. Without their guidance, support, and unwavering belief in my potential, I would not have reached this point of growth and development.

From mentors who generously shared their wisdom and expertise to colleagues who pushed me out of my comfort zone, each person has taught me invaluable lessons about leadership, resilience, and teamwork. It is through their collective encouragement that I have been able to tap into my strengths and passions while also challenging myself to continuously improve. This journey has indeed been a team effort, and I am so incredibly thankful for the myriad of opportunities they have provided me with along the way.

How Has Becoming a Leader Changed My Life?

Being a leader has completely transformed my life in ways I never anticipated.

Firstly, it has enhanced my self-confidence and belief in my abilities. Taking charge of a team or project requires me to make tough decisions and trust myself to lead others effectively. Alongside this newfound confidence, being a leader has taught me the importance of effective communication and collaboration. I have learned how to articulate my ideas clearly and listen actively to others' viewpoints, fostering an environment of mutual understanding and productivity.

Additionally, being a leader has helped me develop strong critical thinking skills. The responsibility of guiding a group through obstacles forces me to think critically and find creative solutions under pressure.

Furthermore, seeing the positive impact I can have on my team's growth and success brings me immense fulfillment.

Overall, being a leader has not only influenced my career but also shaped my personal growth by instilling invaluable qualities such as assertiveness, empathy, resilience, and adaptability - qualities that transcend beyond just the workplace but enrich every aspect of my life.

I Am a Leader

So, let me tell you something about myself: I am a leader. Don't get me wrong; I'm not saying this to boost my ego or seek validation. It is just that throughout my life, whether at work or within my social circles, people have always looked up to me for guidance and direction. It is because I possess certain qualities that inspire others - traits like confidence, empathy, and an unobstructed vision.

But it is not just about being in charge; being a leader means taking responsibility for the well-being of those around you and helping them reach their full potential. I believe in leading by example and fostering an inclusive environment where everyone feels heard and valued. I am enthusiastic about motivating others to succeed and pushing boundaries to achieve greatness together. Being a leader is not an easy task, but the reward of seeing those under your guidance thrive makes every challenge worthwhile.

I Love My Job

Being a leader in my job brings me immense joy and fulfillment. One of the main reasons I love being a leader is the opportunity it provides to inspire and motivate others. I take immense pride in setting a positive example for my colleagues, guiding and supporting them on their professional journeys. Being able to witness their growth and development brings me a deep sense of satisfaction.

Moreover, as a leader, I am entrusted with the responsibility of making important decisions that not only impact individual team members but also contribute to the overall success of the organization. This sense of accountability pushes me to constantly improve myself, enhancing my decision-making skills and strategic thinking abilities.

Additionally, being a leader allows me to foster collaboration among team members and promote an inclusive work environment where everyone feels valued and empowered. The ability to empower others to reach their full potential is truly rewarding, making leadership an incredibly gratifying role for me.

Overall, as a leader in my job, I thrive on the opportunity to make a positive impact on both individuals and the organization as a whole through inspiration, decision-making, collaboration, and empowerment.

I love my job because it allows me to utilize my skills, knowledge, and expertise in a field I am enthusiastic about. As a professional, I am constantly challenged and motivated to learn and grow, which keeps me engaged and excited every day.

Additionally, the sense of fulfillment that comes from helping clients achieve their goals is unparalleled. The opportunity to positively impact someone's life or business is gratifying.

Moreover, collaborating with talented individuals who share the same dedication and commitment towards excellence fosters a collaborative environment where ideas are exchanged freely and innovative solutions are born. This job also offers stability and security, with many opportunities for career progression.

Overall, my job not only provides financial stability but also allows me to pursue personal growth while making a meaningful contribution to society—a combination that makes it genuinely fulfilling.

Transition to Leadership

Finding your Leadership Talent

As I stepped into my first leadership role, I quickly realized that finding my place within the team was critical to success. Through reflection and self-examination, I identified my strengths and areas where I needed improvement as a leader. I then applied this knowledge to build trust and respect with my team by actively listening to their concerns, offering support, and leading by example. It is important to acknowledge that different situations may require different leadership styles, so staying adaptable is critical. By providing clear direction while collaborating with others, I found the balance between being authoritative and approachable.

Ultimately, finding my role as a leader has allowed me to bring out the best in myself and those around me by creating an atmosphere of growth and productivity.

Why I Became a Leader?

I've always wanted to be a leader, you know? I just have this drive inside of me to take charge and make things happen. Whether it's in school projects, group activities, or even just amongst my friends, I'm always the one who steps up and starts organizing everything. I have a natural ability to motivate and inspire others, and it feels incredibly rewarding to see them reach their full potential under my guidance.

Being a leader is not about bossing people around or showing off; it is about serving as a role model, earning the respect of your team, and bringing out the best in everyone. I thrive on the challenges that come with leadership - solving problems, making tough decisions, and fostering collaboration. It is not always easy, but the satisfaction I derive from seeing my team succeed makes every effort worth it. As I move forward in life, whether in academic pursuits or professional endeavors, I aim to continue honing my leadership skills because making a positive impact on those around me is what truly drives me.

Born Leader

A born leader possesses innate traits such as exceptional communication skills, decisiveness, and charisma that help them inspire and guide others towards a common goal. They can motivate and energize their teams, even in the face of adversity. Born leaders also demonstrate strong ethics, integrity and accountability while leading by example.

However, it is important to note that not all leaders are necessarily born; leadership skills are developed through experience, training, and coaching. While individuals may have certain advantages when it comes to leadership abilities due to their natural charisma or critical thinking skills, effective leadership requires effort and practice from everyone. In professional settings, those who aspire to lead should focus on honing these qualities through self-reflection, learning from experiences, seeking feedback from colleagues, and continuously pushing themselves out of their comfort zones.

Am I a Born Leader?

Born leaders have a natural instinct to join employees in a common cause or goal. They know how to influence others to share their purpose and continually encourage others to achieve an objective. After convincing others to strive for a common vision, they outline steps that detail how each member can contribute, maintaining productivity. When conflict arises, they can efficiently mediate the situation by learning about each employee's perspectives and reaching a mutual agreement.

Find a mentor who has demonstrated their leadership capabilities. They will give you advice or share what they have learned over the years. Ask them what difficulties they have faced and how they solved them. Your mentor needs to serve as a guide throughout your career.

Leaders DNA

We all have leadership in our DNA, and it appears in many different forms within our body and mind; the one I want to discuss is the business leadership model. Some people believe leaders are born with charisma, empathy, and self-confidence. Born leaders naturally possess extraordinary qualities that make them more effective. They are also charismatic, self-confident, intelligent, and highly socially aware. You will notice that they naturally get along with others and are great at resolving conflicts.

Born leaders are people with an innate capacity to effectively manage and lead groups of people to achieve collective goals. Instead of learning to become an effective leader, they have the instinctive ability to inspire others and encourage them to follow their vision. Employees feel more comfortable accepting instructions and trusting natural-born leaders. Born leaders can continually improve their leadership by identifying new skills to develop and practicing different management styles.

Why Become a Great Leader

So, you want to be a leader, huh? Here is the deal: becoming a great leader isn't just about bossing people around or having a fancy title. It is about inspiring and motivating others, building strong relationships, and guiding your team towards success.

First things first, hone your communication skills. A great leader knows how to listen actively, express their ideas clearly, and take feedback positively.

Develop empathy, too – understanding your team members' strengths and weaknesses can help you delegate responsibilities effectively.

One crucial trait is leading by example; if you want your team to work hard and be enthusiastic about their tasks, then show them you're willing to put in the effort yourself.

Do not forget to recognize and appreciate your team members' achievements – a little praise goes a long way!

Finally, always strive for personal growth as a leader by seeking feedback from others and continuously learning from your experiences.

How to take control

Here are five tips to help you survive being your best leadership self.

1. Retrain your brain to react as you do once you have solved the problem, that warm feeling or phew that flows through the body.
2. What if everything turns out okay? Just think you have survived every problem that has come your way, so what if you tell yourself what if the worst never happens?
3. Train your brain to stop performing continuous worst-case scenario play in your mind!
4. Spend your brain power and time working on a solution, start fearing the worst, and make yourself feel happy.
5. Stop hearing your team and start listening to your employees.

Great Leaders

Great leaders have an innate desire to learn. They do not need rewards to learn new skills to better themselves and regularly ask questions when they want to know more about a particular topic. Natural-born leaders enjoy learning about different areas of a business to see if they can contribute to a goal or objective.

They encourage others to learn more to help them excel in their careers. When an employee asks about different opportunities within the company, a born leader is eager to find ways for them to learn more about the position and give them the tools they need to succeed.

They have self-confidence.

Self-confidence is fundamental for effective leadership. Making decisions when uncertainty is inevitable, and good leaders take responsibility when choosing an uncertain outcome.

Can You Learn Leadership?

Almost all leadership skills are traits people inherently have, such as empathy and decisiveness. Even if you do not feel like you have those characteristics, you have at least a little inside you. Focusing on bringing them to the surface and strengthening them can help. Other skills, such as communication and active listening, are things you can develop. You can break them down into more minor skills that you learn to improve overall.

Learning leadership qualities is a lifelong journey that requires dedication, self-reflection, and continuous development. One of the fundamental ways to learn leadership skills is through experience, as it provides opportunities to make decisions, take responsibility for outcomes, and interact with others.

Additionally, seeking mentorship from established leaders can be invaluable in gaining insight into effective practices and receiving guidance on specific challenges. Reading books and attending seminars or workshops hosted by renowned experts can also enhance leadership acumen by learning from their experiences and theories.

Furthermore, personal attributes such as emotional intelligence, resilience, and adaptability play a critical role in developing strong leadership capabilities. Reflecting on past experiences and leveraging feedback from peers or superiors helps identify areas for improvement and encourages growth.

Ultimately, mastering leadership traits involves a combination of practical experience, education, self-awareness, and openness to learning from others' successes and failures.

Good Manager vs. A Leader

When comparing a good manager and a leader, it's important to note that they are not mutually exclusive. While a good manager focuses on efficiently executing tasks, meeting targets, and ensuring the smooth functioning of the team or organization, a leader goes beyond these responsibilities. A leader inspires and motivates team members towards a common goal, employing emotional intelligence and fostering trust within the group. They possess excellent communication skills, empathize with their team members' concerns, and encourage open dialogue.

Unlike managers who follow set procedures, leaders challenge the status quo, think creatively, and embrace innovation. They lead by example instead of commanding authority and empower their teams to achieve greatness. Both are crucial for success in different ways – a good manager ensures operational efficiency, while an effective leader inspires individuals to reach their highest potential.

Communication

The Art of Communications

Communication can be called an art as one must use one's personal skill and knowledge to solve many complicated problems to achieve enterprise objectives. Like most arts, Communication is personal in nature in the sense that every manager/person has their own method of communicating. The better your ability to speak with others, the better you will become.

Communication is an art form because it requires the skillful use of language and non-verbal cues to express ideas, emotions, and intentions effectively. Just like a painter uses strokes and colors to create a visual masterpiece, adept communicators carefully choose their words, tone, body language, and even timing to convey a compelling message. Artistic communication involves capturing the audience's attention through storytelling techniques, engaging metaphors, or captivating narratives. It entails listening actively, processing information critically, and responding thoughtfully. Successful communicators can adapt their style to different audiences or contexts while maintaining authenticity. They can effortlessly paint vivid mental pictures, evoke emotion with their words, or inspire action through persuasive speeches.

Furthermore, communication goes beyond conveying information; it enables deep connections between individuals by fostering trust and understanding. By honing their craft over time and continuously refining their skills, skilled communicators can truly master this delicate and nuanced art form in any professional setting.

Leaders Provide Clear Answers and Directions

Clear communication is paramount for a leader in any professional setting. Influential leaders understand that goals cannot be achieved without clear and concise communication, conflicts cannot be resolved, and collaboration among team members cannot occur. Providing clear communication ensures that everyone is on the same page and has a clear understanding of expectations, tasks, and objectives. This allows employees to align their efforts towards achieving shared goals, increasing productivity and efficiency within the workplace.

Additionally, clear communication fosters transparency and trust among team members since they have full visibility into what is expected from them. It also minimizes misunderstandings and errors caused by misinterpretation of information.

Furthermore, when leaders communicate clearly, they demonstrate respect for their subordinates by valuing the time and effort invested in their work.

Overall, clear communication plays a vital role in driving organizational success by establishing an environment where effective teamwork, problem-solving, innovation, and growth can flourish.

Leaders know that they can accomplish goals, so they trust their intuition when they need to make a choice. Self-confidence reassures employees that they are doing the right thing and helps them to have faith in the company's missions and ideals.

They unite employees. Leaders can naturally join employees in a common cause or goal. They know how to influence others to share their purpose and continually encourage others to achieve an objective. After convincing others to strive for a common vision, they outline steps that detail how each member can contribute, maintaining productivity. When conflict arises, they can quickly mediate the situation by learning about each employee's perspectives and reaching a mutual agreement.

How Do Leaders Communicate Their Vision to Their Teams?

Effective communication is key for a leader to successfully relay their vision to their team.

Firstly, clarity is vital. The leader must articulate their vision in a concise and easily understandable manner, ensuring that everyone comprehends the goals. Secondly, a leader must use effective listening skills, taking the time to hear their team members' thoughts and concerns about the vision. This fosters an open and inclusive culture where everyone feels valued and motivated to contribute.

Additionally, employing various communication channels such as face-to-face meetings, memos, or even utilizing technology-driven platforms can help reach broader audiences and ensure the message resonates across different personality types and working preferences. Visual aids such as presentations or charts can enhance comprehension by providing clear visuals accompanying verbal explanations.

Lastly, consistent follow-up is necessary throughout the implementation process on both an individual and team level, providing guidance and reassurance while allowing for any necessary adjustments or feedback. By actively engaging in these practices, leaders can communicate their vision while maintaining a harmonious work environment based on openness and collaboration.

Following the Rules

So, here is the deal - following the rules is pretty darn important. It might seem a bit annoying at times, like when you just want to let loose and do your own thing. But rules are not made to bring you down or ruin your fun; they are designed to keep things running smoothly and ensure everyone's safety and well-being. Think about it - if we had no rules to abide by, chaos would pretty much rule our lives. By sticking to the guidelines set in place, whether at school, work, or even in social settings, we create an environment where people can coexist harmoniously.

Plus, rules often provide a clear structure and help prevent conflicts or misunderstandings.

So, next time you find yourself tempted to bend or break the rules, remember that their purpose is for our collective benefit.

Interpersonal Communication

Working on your communication skills is important when figuring out how to be a great leader. Interpersonal communication includes everything you use to communicate with others, not just your words.

Your tone, body language, facial expressions and hand gestures also impact how your employees receive the verbal messages you give them. Remember, employees infer meaning from your verbal and non-verbal signals, and it is critical to remain aware of both when addressing your team.

Example: If you are kicking off a complicated project with your team and want to help motivate them for the tasks ahead, it is crucial to deliver the message using a positive, upbeat tone, a smile and words like "opportunity" rather than "challenge." Using positive, enthusiastic gestures and maintaining eye contact with your team can also help drum up support for the new project.

Active Listening

Another crucial communication skill every leader should embrace is active listening—in other words, listening carefully to the message the other person is delivering and retaining the information they share. This can help you better understand each team member's personal needs, challenges, and concerns so you can proactively address them. It also enables you to build rapport and leave a positive impression.

Active listening does not mean you always have to agree or give your employees what they ask for, but showing that you are listening, instead of just brushing them off, can help build relationships with your employees.

Example: If a team member shares they want to take on more creative projects, and you begin delegating more creative assignments to them, it shows you are listening to their needs and care about their fulfillment at work.

Leaders Are Great Listeners

Leaders give their full attention to a speaker during a conversation. They are good at maintaining eye contact and expressing an open body language style. When they respond to you, they won't turn the conversation to whatever they want to talk about. They will respond thoughtfully and ask questions to clarify when needed. Great leaders have a genuine interest in the ideas of other people.

They do not overwork themselves.

Phenomenally successful leaders know that work-life balance is something that cannot be neglected. They make time outside of work and personal activities. Taking time for themselves helps them achieve more when they are at work. Since they understand the importance of a healthy work-life balance, they will not overwork their team members. They encourage others to take time away from work when they need it. Knowing when employees need a break shows that they genuinely care for their well-being.

They constantly learn new things.

Listen vs Hearing Me

Listening and hearing are often used interchangeably, but they are not the same. Hearing is a biological process where sound waves enter our ears and are processed by our brains. On the other hand, listening goes beyond just the physical act of hearing. It involves actively paying attention to and comprehending what is being said, which requires focus and concentration. When we listen, we not only hear the words being spoken but also try to understand their meaning, context, and emotions behind them. Listening involves interpreting non-verbal cues like facial expressions and body language, too. It is a skill that can be developed through practice and requires patience and empathy. While hearing is passive, listening is an active process that allows us to engage with others genuinely.

So, next time someone claims they were listening, ensure they were truly doing more than just hearing!

Keep Them Focused

To ensure your staff remains focused, it is crucial to establish a clear and inspiring vision for your organization. Communicating this vision regularly will help align everyone's efforts towards a common goal.

Additionally, providing employees with specific and achievable objectives will enable them to prioritize their tasks effectively. Regularly checking in on progress and offering constructive feedback can further motivate individuals to stay on track. Creating an environment conducive to concentration by minimizing distractions, such as enforcing quiet workspaces or implementing time management techniques like the Pomodoro Technique, can also aid in maintaining focus. Encouraging open communication and fostering a positive team culture will allow employees to seek support when needed and collaborate efficiently.

Furthermore, investing in professional development opportunities will not only enhance individual skills but also demonstrate your commitment to their growth, which can increase dedication and engagement among staff members. By consistently reinforcing the importance of focus and providing the necessary resources and support, you can foster a dedicated workforce capable of achieving optimal results.

Use Stories as a Tool

Using stories to assist staff is an invaluable approach employing empathy and relatability. By sharing firsthand experiences or recounting anecdotes, managers can effectively engage their employees and impart valuable lessons in a way that resonates with them on a human level. Stories have the power to forge connections, inspire action, and promote a deeper understanding of complex issues.

Moreover, they help create a safe environment where individuals can feel comfortable expressing their own concerns, ideas, and aspirations. This storytelling technique enhances communication skills and contributes to team cohesion and trust-building within the workplace.

Additionally, stories allow managers to illustrate abstract concepts or emphasize specific points with concrete examples, making information easier to grasp and remember.

Ultimately, incorporating storytelling into professional interactions fosters an inclusive culture that encourages growth, promotes collaboration, and enhances productivity.

Having Coffee or Lunch

Having coffee or lunch with your team is a wonderful way to foster camaraderie and build strong professional relationships. These informal settings create an opportunity for open communication and can often lead to more productive collaboration in the workplace. Sharing a meal or a cup of coffee allows team members to get to know each other personally, which in turn helps create a positive and supportive work environment. It encourages the exchange of ideas, promotes teamwork, and boosts morale by showing that all team members are valued individuals with unique perspectives.

Furthermore, these casual interactions can also provide an avenue for many mentoring opportunities and knowledge sharing within the team.

Overall, taking the time to have coffee or lunch with your team demonstrates a commitment to building strong working relationships that contribute to the success of the individuals and the entire organization.

Why Have an Open-Door Policy

So, having an open-door policy is the idea of being approachable and accessible to others. It means you are always willing to listen, support, and provide guidance whenever somebody needs it. Adopting this mindset can create an open and inviting environment for everyone involved, whether you are a boss, a teacher, or just a friend. It fosters trust and encourages transparency because people feel comfortable enough to bring up their concerns or share their ideas without fearing judgment or consequences. Plus, it shows that you genuinely care about the well-being and opinions of others – which is incredible if you ask me!

So, next time someone knocks on your door (or virtual chat window), embrace that opportunity with open arms!

Sending Complementary Emails

Sending compliment emails and messages is a fantastic way to brighten someone's day and show appreciation. Whether it is a colleague, friend, or family member, taking the time to acknowledge their hard work, kindness, or talent can go a long way in building strong relationships. When crafting these messages, make sure to be sincere and specific about what you are complimenting them on. This will demonstrate that you genuinely value their efforts.

Also, be mindful of the tone and context of your message - keep it friendly and casual so as not to come across as overly formal or insincere. Remember, a simple word of praise can have a powerful impact on someone's mood and motivation. So do not hesitate to spread some positivity through those virtual compliments!

Always Lead by Example?

Leading by example is effective when it comes to influencing others. When we consistently demonstrate the behavior we want to see in others, it creates a powerful ripple effect. People are more likely to follow our lead if they see us practicing what we preach. By embodying the values, attitudes, and work ethic that we expect from our team, colleagues, or subordinates, we gain their respect and trust.

Moreover, leading by example fosters a sense of accountability within the group because everyone knows they are expected to live up to the same standards. It also inspires and motivates others to improve themselves as they witness firsthand the positive outcomes of emulating exemplary conduct.

Ultimately, leading by example not only helps shape a cohesive and productive environment but also encourages personal growth and development among individuals looking up to us as role models.

Leaders Walk Around

So, let's talk about this whole "lead by walking around" thing. It's a cool concept in leadership where instead of being confined to an office, bosses actively engage with their teams by physically moving around and interacting with them on the work floor. By doing so, leaders can observe firsthand what is happening, get to know their employees on a personal level, and actively foster relationships built on trust and open communication.

Plus, it helps create a positive and inclusive work culture where everyone feels seen and heard. Not only does this approach make leaders more accessible, but it also allows for real-time problem-solving and the opportunity to provide immediate feedback or recognition.

So, if you are looking for a way to be a more effective leader while creating an awesome work environment, give "lead by walking around" a shot!

How Can You Improve Your Leadership Skills?

If you are not sure how to become a better leader, start with a self-evaluation to determine how well you are doing with different leadership skills. Identify the skills you want to improve based on that reflection and make a conscious effort to improve in those areas.

For example, if you need to work on active listening, be aware of how well you are doing with listening in every interaction you have, even those outside of work.

You can also ask your employees or acquaintances for feedback on specific skills. They might have insight that can help you improve. For some skills, such as conflict resolution, you can take classes to learn specific skills and strategies. Practice implementing the skills you learn as you interact with your team.

What Else Can You Do to Become a Better Leader?

Some other things you can do to become a better leader include:

- Continue learning through additional degrees or training programs.
- Find a mentor who embodies the type of leadership you want to display and learn from them.
- Ask for feedback regularly from other leaders and your employees.
- Evaluate your leadership style to understand what works best for you and identify potential problems with how you lead.
- Experiment with new things all the time to find the best strategies for you.
- Understand the expectations of your role to help you determine if you are meeting them.

Devastating Events While in Management

Leading is a multifaceted responsibility that demands impeccable decision-making skills, resilience, and composure. However, even the most experienced leaders may face devastating events that challenge their leadership abilities. Such events can range from natural disasters that wreak havoc on infrastructure to unexpected economic downturns that cripple organizations. During these trying times, leaders must exhibit unwavering strength and determination while maintaining empathy for those affected. Effective communication becomes paramount as leaders must address concerns, rally teams, and create a sense of stability amidst the chaos.

Additionally, they must remain adaptable, quickly devising new strategies and approaches to mitigate damages and ensure the long-term survival of their organization. Leading through devastating events requires a delicate balance of decisiveness, compassion, and flexibility to guide the team towards recovery while instilling confidence in uncertain times.

Yelling at Staff

In a professional setting, it is crucial to recognize that yelling never achieves the desired outcomes. While shouting may create an immediate stoppage or attention, it fails to foster effective communication or encourage long-term behavior change. Yelling typically evokes fear, defensiveness, and demoralization among individuals involved, hindering collaboration and inhibiting productive work relationships.

Instead of resorting to raising one's voice, professionals should strive for open dialogue and active listening as key elements of successful communication. By adopting a calm and composed tone, professionals can address issues constructively while showing respect for others' perspectives. Employing alternative conflict-resolution strategies such as mediation or compromise allows for better problem-solving. It also promotes a positive work culture built on trust and understanding.

In sum, eliminating yelling from the workplace reinforces professionalism, promotes healthier relationships amongst colleagues, and enhances overall productivity within the organization.

All Ages Can Show Leadership Qualities

Let me tell you about my four-year-old grandson, who is quite the little leader. From a young age, he has displayed a natural ability to take charge and inspire those around him.

Whether it's organizing games with his friends at the school or making up imaginative stories during playtime, he always seems to be at the center of the action. His confidence and charisma draw others to him, and they eagerly follow his lead. It's truly remarkable to see such leadership qualities in someone so young, and I have no doubt that he will continue to grow and thrive as a leader in whatever path he chooses to pursue in life.

Even Toddlers Show Early Signs

Toddlers, you know, those little pint-sized bundles of energy, have an uncanny ability to get their way. It is like they possess a secret superpower specifically designed to manipulate and charm us adults into doing their bidding. But why is this the case? Well, it all boils down to a combination of factors.

Firstly, toddlers have an innate sense of persistence and determination that rivals even the most resolute marathon runner. They simply do not give up easily when it comes to getting what they want.

Additionally, their adorable cherubic faces tug at our heartstrings, making it incredibly difficult to say no. Let us not forget about their expert-level negotiation skills - who knew such tiny humans could bargain so effectively? Whether it's using their limited vocabulary or cleverly employing tantrums as a last-ditch effort, toddlers sure know how to play the game.

So, next time you find yourself wondering why your little munchkin always seems to get their way, just remember, they have mastered the art of persuasion with their irresistible combination of determination, cuteness overload, and strategic tactics.

Toddlers are adept at getting their way due to a combination of factors rooted in their developmental stage and behavioral patterns.

Firstly, toddlers have an innate sense of determination and persistence that drives them to achieve their immediate goals. Their brains are rapidly developing during this time, facilitating learning and critical thinking skills, which they effectively employ to manipulate situations into favorable outcomes.

Furthermore, toddlers possess limited impulse control and often lack the ability to regulate their emotions appropriately, resulting in temper tantrums or persistent demands until they achieve the desired result. They also thrive on attention and learn quickly that certain behaviors elicit responses from adults, allowing them to exploit adult vulnerabilities through manipulation strategies such as negotiating or using cuteness.

Additionally, toddlers lack a comprehensive understanding of consequences and, thus, are less deterred by potential negative outcomes when attempting to get their way. These factors combined establish a compelling case for why toddlers demonstrate remarkable proficiency in ensuring their desires are met.

Calm Staff Down

When faced with angry employees, it is crucial to handle the situation professionally and effectively.

Firstly, it is essential to create a calm and safe environment by finding a quiet space where both parties can speak without interruptions. Active listening plays a vital role in diffusing anger. Allow employees to vent their frustrations and concerns while maintaining an empathetic and non-judgmental attitude. It is also important to recognize and validate their emotions, showing that you understand their perspective.

Next, engage in open communication by asking probing questions to gain clarity on the underlying issues. This demonstrates your willingness to solve problems collaboratively. Ensure that their concerns will be addressed promptly while proposing realistic solutions or compromises where applicable.

Lastly, document the conversation for future reference and follow up with actions agreed upon during the discussion to rebuild trust with employees and ensure a positive work environment moving forward.

Can Team Meetings Work

Team meetings can be an effective tool for fostering collaboration, communication, and productivity within a professional setting. When facilitated correctly, team meetings provide a platform for sharing ideas, clarifying objectives, and addressing concerns. They allow team members to collectively brainstorm solutions and provide input on initiatives or projects.

Moreover, team meetings promote transparency and accountability as progress updates can be shared, allowing everyone to understand their role in achieving organizational goals.

Additionally, these meetings enable teams to establish a sense of camaraderie as they work towards a common purpose. However, team meetings must be well-structured and focused to ensure maximum efficiency. This includes setting clear agendas beforehand and inviting only relevant participants. The meeting facilitator needs to keep discussions on track while encouraging active participation from all attendees.

Additionally, regular follow-ups are necessary to assess the effectiveness of implemented solutions and ascertain if further action is required.

Overall, when executed thoughtfully using best practices, team meetings can significantly contribute to a high-performing professional environment.

Leader's Tools

Never Forget Good Customer Service

Good customer service is essential in maintaining a positive business image and building long-lasting customer relationships. It goes beyond simply fulfilling their needs; it involves anticipating their expectations and going the extra mile to meet and exceed them. Professional customer service representatives are knowledgeable about their products or services, enabling them to provide accurate information and guidance to customers. They also possess excellent communication skills, actively listening to customer queries or concerns and responding promptly and courteously.

Furthermore, a professional tone of voice is crucial in customer interactions, ensuring that all conversations are respectful and maintain a sense of professionalism. Good customer service professionals take ownership of any issues that arise and work towards resolving them in a timely manner, demonstrating accountability for their actions. By consistently delivering exceptional customer service, businesses can establish themselves as trustworthy and reliable providers in their respective industries.

Always be on the Alert for Bad Customer Service

Bad customer service refers to a substandard level of assistance or support provided by an organization to its customers. It is characterized by a lack of empathy, communication gaps, and disregard for customer needs and expectations. This can manifest in several ways: long waiting times, untrained or unhelpful staff, unresolved complaints, or a general lack of attention to detail.

Besides, bad customer service not only tarnishes a company's reputation but also leads to dissatisfied customers who are more likely to take their business elsewhere. This detrimental aspect is particularly concerning given the age of social media and online reviews, where negative experiences can quickly spread like wildfire, impacting potential sales and brand perception. Thus, companies should prioritize providing exceptional customer service through well-trained and attentive employees who go above and beyond to resolve issues promptly and effectively.

A Leader Manages and Follows the Process

Managing the process is a crucial aspect of any project or organizational management. It involves understanding and adhering to the established procedures, policies, and guidelines that inform the workflow, communication, and decision-making processes involved in achieving specific objectives. This approach requires effective planning, execution, monitoring, control, and evaluation of every step along the way to ensure that each task contributes optimally towards the overarching goals. To manage towards the process entails forethought and familiarity with best practices in project management, including resource allocation, risk identification and mitigation strategies, as well as performance measurement techniques that enable adaptation to changing circumstances with minimal disruption. It also requires clear communication channels within teams for timely coordination of efforts and efficient resolution of obstacles along the way. In implementing this approach effectively, organizations can enhance efficiencies in their operations, resulting in increased productivity while achieving higher quality outcomes within shorter timelines.

One of my favorite management tools is managing the process, which is your standard operations procedures. Many employees want to work hard and be successful, but without specific training, they will only fail. Many Leaders think if you show an employee how to do a job once or twice, the employee will catch on and become successful.

This type of thinking causes concerns such as slowing down your daily business and impeding your culture. The way to help your new employee succeed is to create tools to help the employee succeed. Managing the process of any project requires a level of professionalism, organization, and critical thinking. It is essential to approach every step strategically and establish clear goals, timelines, and metrics for success. This involves creating a plan that considers potential risks and obstacles and identifying necessary resources such as personnel or technology tools.

Additionally, effective communication with stakeholders is vital to ensure everyone is on the same page and understands roles and expectations. Regular progress updates can help alleviate potential issues before they become more significant problems. A professional manager should also lead by example by delegating tasks effectively while allowing team members autonomy in their work process and providing guidance as needed. Effective process management ensures project outcomes align with organizational objectives while minimizing delays or errors along the way.

The Importance of Today's Lists

Let us talk about the importance of to-do lists. They may seem like a small thing, but trust me, they can make a world of difference in our busy lives. Primarily, having a to-do list helps us stay organized and focused. By jotting down tasks that need our attention, we prioritize them and avoid forgetting important stuff. It is like having your personal roadmap for the day or week ahead. Secondly, ticking off items on a to-do list gives us a sense of accomplishment. There is something immensely satisfying about crossing completed tasks off that paper or digital checklist! It boosts our productivity and motivation levels as we move forward with a clear plan in mind.

Lastly, let us not forget how to-do lists reduce stress levels. When everything is laid out in front of us, we can visualize what needs to be done without feeling overwhelmed by everything cluttering our minds. So go ahead, grab that pen, and start making your very own to-do list. Do not forget today's to-do list is tomorrow's accomplishments.

A Leaders Golden Rule

The golden rules of leadership are essential principles that guide individuals in successfully leading others.

Firstly, effective communication is a fundamental aspect of leadership. Leaders must clearly articulate their vision, goals, and expectations to ensure everyone is on the same page.

Moreover, leaders must actively listen to their team members and provide constructive feedback. Second, integrity plays a pivotal role in leadership. Leaders should always demonstrate honesty and transparency while upholding high ethical standards. By setting an example through their actions, leaders gain the trust and respect of their followers.

Additionally, cultivating a positive work environment fosters motivation and productivity among employees. Great leaders create a culture of inclusivity where every team member feels valued and appreciated for their contributions.

Lastly, successful leaders never stop learning and developing themselves. They continuously seek knowledge through reading books and attending seminars or workshops to improve their skills and expand their understanding of the world around them.

In conclusion, these golden rules form the foundation for effective leadership by emphasizing communication, integrity, creating a positive work environment, and continuous personal growth.

Leadership is Not Easy

Leadership is a complex and nuanced practice requiring diverse skills and qualities to guide teams or organizations towards success effectively.

One of the most prominent challenges leaders face today is the changing landscape of modern business, including technological advancements, globalization, and shifting workforce demographics. Effective leadership now involves building and maintaining diverse teams while cultivating creativity, innovation, and adaptability in response to rapidly evolving market conditions. This type of leadership requires individuals who can balance operational efficiency with strategic visioning, engage employees through effective communication and empowerment, manage conflict effectively to drive positive outcomes and maintain a deep commitment to ethical decision-making practices.

It takes time, experience, and skill development for any leader to excel in all these areas. As such, leadership is difficult because it demands constant adaptation and learning - an ability that many may not possess right away.

A Leader is a Teacher

Being a leader who also takes on the role of a teacher is crucial for fostering growth, development, and overall success within a team or organization. When leaders become teachers, they empower those around them with knowledge and skills that enable individuals to continuously learn and improve. Teachers lead by example, demonstrating the values, behaviors, and attitudes they expect from their team members. They create a learning environment where mistakes are seen as opportunities for growth rather than failures. By sharing wisdom, experience, and expertise with their team members through effective mentorship and coaching, leaders can inspire trust, build confidence, and motivate individuals to reach their full potential.

Additionally, leaders as teachers encourage open communication, provide constructive feedback and tailor learning experiences to meet individual needs. This approach promotes collaboration and teamwork while reinforcing the pursuit of continuous improvement.

Ultimately, being a leader who serves as a teacher fosters an environment of growth mindset that enhances performance outcomes for both individuals and the entire team.

Leaders Control Their Environment

When we try to be effective in what we must do as a leader, when trying to be productive or—from a wider perspective—try to be happy, we are accustomed to acting on the factors that we can control and keep our fingers crossed so that other environmental factors we can't control shows up, or at least turn out not to become hostile.

Nonetheless, it seems that we can do more. It turns out that many of the things that happen to us, things that we just complain about because we believe we can do nothing to avoid them, can be controlled indirectly. It turns out that your effectiveness in life is based to a great extent on the level of control that you can exert on your surroundings.

Obviously, they are completely beyond our control. However, people who go through one tough situation after another tend to be people unable to control their surroundings. Similarly, highly competent people in whatever aspect of life tend to possess a great capacity to avoid or minimize negative external factors and to cause and maximize positive external factors.

Leaders Must Allow Others to Lead

Effective leaders understand the importance of autonomy and empowerment in fostering team growth and development. They recognize that true leadership is not about exerting control or micromanaging but rather about enabling others to step into leadership roles themselves. Leaders allow others to lead when they have confidence in their team members' abilities and trust in their decision-making skills. This involves delegating tasks and responsibilities, providing guidance and support when needed, but also giving individuals the freedom to make decisions independently. By doing so, leaders create a culture of ownership and accountability where employees feel valued and empowered, leading to increased motivation, innovation, and productivity.

Furthermore, allowing others to lead allows leaders themselves to focus on strategic thinking, problem-solving, and long-term visioning while building a diverse pipeline of future leaders capable of driving organizational success beyond individual capabilities.

How Does a Leader Stay Motivated?

Staying motivated as a leader can be quite challenging at times, but keeping the fire burning is crucial. One key aspect is setting clear goals and envisioning the desired future outcome. By constantly reminding yourself of these goals and focusing on the bigger picture, you'll find renewed purpose and motivation.

Another helpful strategy is surrounding yourself with a supportive and positive network of individuals who inspire you. Engaging in open conversations, seeking feedback, and learning from their experiences will help fuel your motivation. It is also important to have a healthy work-life balance to prevent burnout. Taking breaks, pursuing personal passions, or spending quality time with loved ones can recharge your batteries and maintain your drive.

Lastly, acknowledging achievements and celebrating milestones along the way enables you to stay motivated by recognizing progress made towards your ultimate vision. Remember that motivation comes from within, so take care of yourself mentally and physically – ensuring a positive mindset will help you lead more effectively.

How Does a Leader Stand Firm?

Being a leader requires the ability to stand firm, even in the face of challenges and adversity. One way a leader can achieve this is by having unwavering convictions that align with their values and beliefs. By having an unobstructed vision and staying true to it, they can withstand external pressures or temptations that may compromise their integrity.

Another crucial aspect is effective communication skills - a strong leader knows how to convey their thoughts and ideas firmly yet respectfully. Confidence also plays a significant role in standing firm as a leader; when leaders exude self-assurance, it inspires confidence in their followers as well.

Moreover, leaders must be adaptable and willing to make tough decisions while considering various perspectives. They should seek feedback from others but trust themselves enough to make difficult choices when necessary.

Ultimately, being consistent in actions and decisions reinforces the leader's stance and earns them respect from those they lead.

The Leadership Hero

A "leader hero" is a term used to describe a leader who possesses exceptional qualities of leadership and heroism. These individuals are characterized by their ability to inspire and motivate others, act with unwavering integrity and courage in the face of adversity and possess an unrelenting commitment to achieving meaningful results. They lead by example, setting lofty standards for themselves and their teams while fostering an environment of trust, collaboration, and innovation. As a result, they can build strong relationships with their followers, earning their respect and loyalty over time. This leadership style is particularly effective during times of change or uncertainty when individuals need stability and guidance from someone they can trust to navigate challenging circumstances.

Overall, the "leader hero" embodies the essence of ultimate leadership - inspiring others to be their best selves while pursuing a common goal with unwavering dedication and determination. Knowing oneself is a complex and continuous process that requires self-awareness, introspection, and honesty. To truly know oneself in a professional context, it is crucial to understand one's strengths, weaknesses, values, and goals. This understanding should be informed by objective feedback from others as well as firsthand experiences. People who know themselves professionally know what motivates them, what their working style is like, and how they can effectively communicate with and work alongside others. This knowledge allows them to make informed decisions about career goals and paths, take ownership of their successes and failures, seek outgrowth opportunities that align with their values and interests, and build a fulfilling career. Developing such self-awareness requires intentional reflection on past experiences and ongoing learning opportunities, both formally and informally, to continue developing skills necessary for success while assessing internal motivations through the lens of bringing awareness within the profession, which helps individuals know themselves better professionally.

Goal Setting

One of the most challenging obstacles leaders face is unifying their team around a common purpose and driving cooperation. Setting clear, measurable goals helps teams work together, and getting employees involved in setting goals can get them to invest more in achieving them.

You also need to communicate those goals clearly and ensure everyone understands their part in accomplishing them. When they achieve their objective, it helps them bond over a shared success.

Example: Instead of telling your team you want to increase revenue this quarter, set an exact goal with a measurable number. Then, lay out a clear roadmap for reaching it. This way, your team knows what is expected and can unite to meet the objective. You might also get input from your employees to see what they think is a reasonable revenue goal.

Mastering Your Department

As a leader, it is essential to possess a deep understanding and proficiency in your department's knowledge. Knowledge of the specific domain allows you to make informed decisions, guide and mentor your team effectively, and set realistic goals and expectations. It also instills confidence in your team members, who rely on you for guidance and support. Having expertise in your department ensures that you can provide valuable insights during discussions or strategic planning sessions, leading to better outcomes for the organization.

Additionally, being knowledgeable about the latest trends and advancements in your field positions you to identify potential opportunities or risks before they arise.

In summary, mastering the knowledge of your department not only enhances your leadership abilities but also enables you to drive success within your team and organization.

The Best Leaders Know

Becoming a leader requires a combination of inherent qualities, dedicated effort, and continuous growth. To start on this path, one must possess effective communication skills, the ability to inspire and motivate others, as well as excellent decision-making abilities.

Additionally, fostering emotional intelligence is crucial for effective leadership, enabling one to understand and empathize with team members' perspectives. Leaders are also known for their integrity and ethical behavior, consistently demonstrating honesty and transparency in their actions. However, true leaders do not rest on their laurels; they actively seek opportunities for growth through learning from mentors or by pursuing formal education in leadership development programs. Great leaders recognize the importance of self-awareness and introspection, constantly evaluating their strengths, weaknesses, and areas of improvement to refine their skills further. Flexibility and adaptability are critical traits for leaders navigating dynamic professional environments.

Ultimately, becoming a leader is an ongoing journey that demands dedication to personal growth while prioritizing the success of those under your guidance.

Tools a Leader Can Use

So, let us talk about why a leader needs tools to improve. Being a leader is not just about giving orders or making decisions; it is about inspiring and empowering others to work together towards a common goal. And to do that effectively, leaders need the right tools. These tools can come in various forms - from communication tools that help keep everyone on the same page to project management tools that streamline processes and improve efficiency. By utilizing these tools, leaders can enhance their decision-making abilities, communicate more effectively with their team, and stay organized amidst the chaos of day-to-day operations.

Additionally, these tools also enable leaders to gather data and analyze trends, which can aid in identifying areas for improvement and making informed strategies. So, whether it is software applications or mental frameworks, having the right set of tools as a leader significantly contributes to personal and organizational development.

Leadership and Customer Service

A leader is essential to providing excellent customer service. A good leader understands the importance of building strong customer relationships and sets the example for their team. They are attentive to customers' needs, ensuring open lines of communication and actively seeking feedback. This allows them to address any concerns promptly and find innovative solutions to improve their services.

Additionally, a leader fosters a positive work environment by showing appreciation for their team's efforts and empowering them to make decisions that benefit the customer. They provide ongoing training and support so employees feel confident handling various customer situations independently. A successful leader prioritizes customer satisfaction and encourages a culture of empathy and understanding among employees, which leads to loyal customers who trust the company's commitment to exceptional service.

Can Leaders Fail?

Can a leader fail to connect with his staff? Absolutely! It is like trying to microwave pasta without water – it just will not work. Connecting with your staff is crucial in fostering a positive work environment and ensuring productivity. A leader who fails to establish this connection risks creating an atmosphere of apathy and disengagement among their team members. When there is a lack of connection, employees may feel undervalued, ignored, and deprived of the support they need to thrive in their roles. Communication breakdowns become common, leading to misunderstandings, decreased motivation, and even increased turnover rates within the organization.

So yes, if a leader wants to succeed and build a formidable team, they better put on their social hat and forge those connections with their staff pronto!

The Upside and Downside of Leadership

One of your most challenging leadership positions is the employee's emotional upside and downside of the mountain. As the charts show, employees are mostly excited and motivated when they start a position. Many employees find supporting the upside impossible and will begin looking for reasons to slide down the mountain. This is where you, as the leader, come into action: on good days, bad days, or busy days, you are responsible for motivating your team. Your duty as the leader is to keep your team focused and remain on the upside of the slope. There will be times when you agree with your team and times when you need emotional support. However, the absolute best way to manage this is to remain positive at all costs. Fake it until you make it; remember, your staff is always watching you and taking their lead from you. Your positive reactions will pull your team up the mountain until they can climb on their own again. In the professional realm, a leader must always strive to remain positive to inspire and motivate their team effectively. Positivity serves as a powerful tool in maintaining a productive work environment, encouraging cooperation, creativity, and problem-solving. By approaching challenges with an optimistic mindset, leaders can instill confidence within their teams while fostering resilience during challenging times. A positive leader not only boosts morale but also cultivates a sense of trust among team members, enabling open communication and collaboration. They create an atmosphere encouraging employee growth and development by providing constructive feedback and recognizing achievements.

Moreover, remaining positive enables leaders to navigate obstacles gracefully and find opportunities amidst adversity, leading by example for their team members.

Overall, the ability of a leader to maintain positivity inspires authenticity, fosters teamwork, and drives success in the professional world.

Those Who Will Not Follow the Leader

Leading those who refuse to follow can be a challenging task. Still, with the right approach, it is possible to navigate through this situation effectively. First and foremost, as a leader, it is vital to understand the underlying reasons behind their resistance and address them accordingly. Initiate open and honest conversations to gain insights into their concerns and frustrations. This will help build trust and allow you to tailor your leadership style to accommodate their needs better. Effective communication becomes paramount here - clearly articulate expectations, goals, and the organization's vision while providing rationale behind decisions made. Treat these individuals with respect and empathy, acknowledging their unique perspectives while ensuring accountability.

Additionally, seek opportunities for collaboration and provide avenues where they can contribute their talents or ideas within the boundaries of collective objectives.

Lastly, leading by example demonstrates integrity, transparency, and consistency in your own actions to inspire confidence in following your lead, even for those initially resistant.

Retaining Your Leverage

When it comes to managing your staff, one thing you should always keep in mind is to maintain leverage. And by that, I mean having the upper hand in terms of authority and control.

Now, before you start picturing yourself as some kind of power-hungry dictator, let me clarify what I mean by leverage in a more casual tone. It is not about being bossy or ruling with an iron fist at all. It's about building healthy relationships based on trust and respect while ensuring effective communication and productivity. By maintaining leverage, you are focusing on empowering your staff to perform at their best while having clear expectations set in place. It means offering support and guidance when needed while holding them accountable for their actions. Doing so creates a harmonious work environment where everyone feels valued and motivated to give their all.

Remember, it is not about being the big bad boss but about leading by example and fostering growth within your team.

Sometimes, a Leader is a Chef

Just like a chef, a leader must possess the skills to plan and execute tasks flawlessly to achieve success. A great leader, just like an exceptional chef, understands the importance of delegation and teamwork. They are responsible for bringing together different ingredients or team members, blending their unique talents and skills to create something extraordinary.

Similarly, leaders need to have an unobstructed vision and the ability to articulate it effectively, much like how chefs communicate their recipes to their teams. A successful leader also knows how to inspire and motivate others, just as a talented chef can ignite passion in their kitchen crew. They both understand that individual contributions are important but work best when everyone feels valued and supported. Both leaders and chefs strive for excellence by continuously learning from failures and adapting their strategies - whether experimenting with new flavors or polishing leadership techniques.

Good Guy vs Bad Guy

In certain circumstances, the depiction of a leader as a villain can have positive implications for both the individual and the organization they lead.

Firstly, it serves as an opportunity for introspection and reflection, allowing the leader to critically evaluate their actions and decision-making processes. By being aware of the perceptions held by others, leaders can identify areas of improvement and implement necessary changes to build trust and collaboration within the team.

Additionally, being depicted as a villain can foster a sense of unity among subordinates who may rally together to overcome challenges or adversities their leader poses. This shared adversity allows for collective problem-solving and encourages individuals to take ownership of their roles, resulting in stronger teams that are resilient and adaptable in the face of challenges. This perception provides an opportunity for self-growth while nurturing a supportive and cohesive work environment conducive to achieving common goals. If you think back to the movies you have seen or books you have read, a great villain has made for a good read or watch.

Why Should a Leader Have a Succession Plan?

Having a secession plan is crucial for any leader, regardless of the scale of their organization or group. It provides a sense of security and preparedness in case unforeseen circumstances arise that could jeopardize the stability or continuity of their leadership. A well-thought-out secession plan ensures a smooth transition of power. It minimizes potential disruptions or conflicts within the team. It also allows the leader to develop and groom potential successors, nurturing a culture of growth and development within the organization. By having a clear succession plan, leaders can build trust among their team members, demonstrating their commitment to ensuring sustainable leadership beyond themselves.

Additionally, it encourages leaders to focus on long-term goals and visions rather than becoming complacent with their position to inspire future leaders with a shared vision and passion for success. Therefore, a succession plan not only safeguards against unexpected incidents but also fosters an environment conducive to effective leadership development and growth.

Warming Up on the Bench

I have experienced, on many occasions, employees I have helped succeed grow a new mindset in which they will believe they are better than you and decide to come after you or your position. Always expect this and be prepared so you are not overtaken or surprised. You may find this hard to deal with, but it is the best compliment you can receive if you make your job seem easy or you are humble during your training with employees.

As a younger leader, I panicked, and I took this personally. As I grew, I realized that these individuals are good or exceptionally good, but it took your greatness to teach and coach these individuals. This is why you must stay on top of your game. It is like sports; the person sitting on the bench wants to replace you.

So, why is the person you are training gunning for your job? Competition in the workplace is inevitable, and it is no surprise that ambitious individuals would seize every opportunity to climb up the career ladder. Your colleague sees your position as a steppingstone to further their professional growth. They may be eager to prove themselves capable of handling higher responsibilities or seeking recognition from superiors. It does not necessarily mean they have ill intentions or want to see you fail miserably. It could just reflect their own aspirations and drive to excel in their chosen field. Having someone who strives to surpass you can serve as a motivating factor for continuous improvement and innovation, pushing both parties to become better versions of themselves.

Competitive Outlook

A true leader in any professional setting understands the value of a competitive team and possesses the necessary skills to foster such an environment.

Firstly, they comprehend that a competitive team drives innovation, productivity, and growth within an organization. To achieve this, a leader establishes clear goals and expectations for each team member, ensuring their roles align with their strengths and interests. They encourage healthy competition among individuals by acknowledging and rewarding outstanding performance.

Moreover, a competent leader emphasizes collaboration rather than fostering an atmosphere of cut-throat competition. They create opportunities for teamwork and mutual support, fostering a sense of camaraderie while pushing individuals to constantly improve themselves.

Additionally, strong leaders invest time and effort into ongoing training and development programs for their team members. By providing them with the knowledge and skills to excel in their roles, leaders enable their teams to stay up-to-date with industry trends and remain at the forefront of their field. A leader who successfully makes his team competitive cultivates an environment where individuals strive for excellence while working together toward common goals—a recipe for long-term success in any professional setting.

You Cannot be a Friend and Boss

Being both a friend and a boss can be incredibly challenging and, often, unrealistic. While having a close relationship with your employees may seem like the ideal situation, blurring the line between friendship and authority can lead to conflicts and favoritism. As a boss, it is crucial to maintain objectivity, make tough decisions, and enforce rules that are in the company's best interest. However, when you are friends with your subordinates, these responsibilities become difficult to fulfill as personal biases may cloud judgement.

Moreover, being too casual or lenient with employees can undermine your position of authority and hinder productivity in the workplace. Building professional relationships built on respect and clear boundaries is essential for effective leadership while fostering positive and cordial interactions with colleagues outside of work hours.

What Separates a Leader from a Friend?

In the realm of professional relationships, what distinguishes a leader from a friend lies in the balance between objectives and personal connections. While both play critical roles in fostering collaboration and productivity, a leader must prioritize organizational goals above personal preferences or biases, exhibiting impartiality and objectivity. They can make tough decisions for the greater good, even if it means sacrificing personal relationships or causing temporary discomfort.

On the other hand, a friend tends to prioritize emotional connection and personal harmony above all else, often avoiding confrontation or difficult conversations that might hinder their relationship. Unlike leaders who maintain a certain level of authority and responsibility over their subordinates' success, friends primarily focus on providing emotional support and camaraderie. Maintaining this distinction allows leaders to inspire and motivate teams towards shared goals while preserving personal boundaries that do not affect the effectiveness of their roles.

Your Staff Forgets You Were Once Them

Do you know what is really amusing sometimes? When your staff seems to completely forget that you were once in their position. I mean, come on, guys, don't act like I never had to answer phones, file paperwork, and deal with annoying customers! It's like they think I just magically appeared in this fancy corner office with a plush chair and a private bathroom. But let me tell you, my friends, I have been through it all. I have made the coffee runs, survived the never-ending meetings, and even had my fair share of rookie mistakes.

So, next time someone from my team feels too entitled or complains about their workload, they should remember where they came from – because that high horse they are riding on is certainly not sustainable.

Dress Attire

Business casual attire is a crucial factor in a supervisor's success. While the notion of dress code may seem trivial, it sets the tone for professionalism and credibility within a workplace. Dressing casually yet appropriately helps to create a comfortable but not overly relaxed environment, fostering open communication and approachability. Supervisors who adhere to a business casual dress code demonstrate respect for both their position and their subordinates, showing that they take their role seriously.

Moreover, dressing professionally enhances one's personal brand and can significantly impact how colleagues, superiors, and clients perceive them. It conveys an image of competence, reliability, and attention to detail—one that translates directly into improved business relationships and increased opportunities for professional growth. Therefore, understanding and implementing the principles of business casual is not just a matter of style but plays a vital part in bolstering a supervisor's overall success.

Join Organizations that Make You a Better Leader

If you want to enhance your leadership skills, one of the best ways is by joining organizations that can provide you with many growth opportunities. Whether it is a professional association, a civic group, or even a sports team, being a part of these groups allows you to collaborate with diverse individuals with varying skill sets and knowledge. Such interactions not only broaden your perspectives but also serve as valuable learning experiences. These organizations often offer leadership training programs, workshops, and mentorship opportunities that can further polish your abilities.

Additionally, actively participating in these groups allows you to practice key leadership traits such as communication, decision-making, and problem-solving on a regular basis.

Ultimately, surrounding yourself with like-minded individuals equally motivated to become better leaders creates an environment conducive to personal and professional development in an organic and enjoyable manner.

How Do Leaders Sleep at Night?

Well, let us start by saying that leaders are human beings, too, and just like everyone else, they need their fair share of shut-eye. But the truth is, the ability of a leader to sleep at night is often influenced by a multitude of factors unique to their position. The weight of responsibility and the constant decision-making can certainly disrupt their restful slumber from time to time. Add to that the pressure of maintaining a high standard, meeting deadlines, and ensuring team success. Unsurprisingly, leaders may occasionally find themselves tangled up in a web of restless thoughts when they hit the pillow. However, strong leaders also possess a remarkable skill: they can compartmentalize their worries and remain focused on long-term goals. They understand the significance of self-care and stress management techniques such as meditation or exercise, which can help them unwind before bedtime.

Moreover, effective communication and delegating tasks to capable team members allow leaders to trust others' abilities while promoting organizational productivity. So yes, even though sometimes it might be tough for leaders to catch some Zs under all that pressure, they have mastered the art of navigating turbulent seas – ensuring both personal well-being and professional achievements along the way.

Emotions

Leaders Always Find Time for Family

Leaders who are dedicated to their roles also recognize the importance of maintaining a healthy work-life balance by finding time for family. Despite the demands and pressures that come with being in leadership positions, effective leaders understand that nurturing personal relationships is crucial for overall well-being and success. By carving out quality time with family members, leaders not only demonstrate their commitment to those who matter most to them but also prioritize self-care and stress management. They comprehend that flourishing both professionally and personally requires a harmonious integration of various aspects of life, including spending precious moments with loved ones. This enables them to recharge, gain perspective, and develop authentic connections outside the workplace.

Furthermore, leaders who are available for family exhibit empathy and emotional intelligence as they cherish the value of human relationships beyond professional achievements. By exemplifying this behavior, inspiring leaders set a positive example for their teams, encouraging others to also cultivate meaningful connections in their own lives.

A Leader's Health is Extremely Important

A leader's health is of utmost importance in professional settings. A leader's physical and mental well-being directly impacts their ability to make sound decisions, effectively communicate with team members, and manage the daily stresses of a demanding job. When leaders prioritize their health, they set an example for others to follow. Physical fitness not only increases energy levels but also improves focus and concentration, allowing leaders to tackle challenges with clarity and determination.

Moreover, leaders who take care of their mental health can maintain a positive outlook even during difficult times, serving as resilient pillars that inspire and motivate their teams.

Additionally, good health fosters strong leadership qualities such as self-discipline and perseverance while reducing absenteeism due to illness or burnout. In conclusion, by valuing their own wellness, leaders uphold standards that promote productivity, establish trust within their teams, and contribute to the overall success of an organization.

Stop Regretting the Past

Regretting the past can be a hindrance to personal growth and professional success. Constantly dwelling on past mistakes and missed opportunities only consumes valuable mental and emotional energy that could be better spent on productive endeavors. Instead of fixating on the past, professionals should utilize their time and resources to focus on the present and future. By acknowledging past experiences as learning opportunities, individuals can gain valuable insights that help them make better choices moving forward. Regret often breeds negativity and self-doubt and reduces confidence, all of which are detrimental to professional development. Embracing a forward-thinking mindset allows professionals to adopt resilience and adaptability in facing challenges. It enables them to cultivate constructive habits like problem-solving, decision-making, and setting realistic goals, which are essential for achieving sustainable success in their chosen field.

Moreover, by letting go of regret, one cultivates a more positive outlook that not only benefits themselves but also positively influences team dynamics and workplace culture. So, it is crucial for professionals to redirect their energy from regret towards self-improvement and future accomplishments to foster personal growth and unlock their full potential.

Stop Worrying about the Future

In today's fast-paced and unpredictable world, we commonly find ourselves consumed by worries and anxieties about the future. However, professionals must recognize the detrimental effects of excessive worry and instead focus on present-day tasks and goals. Constantly obsessing over what may lie ahead can hinder productivity, creativity, and overall job performance. By diverting attention away from the present moment, professionals risk missing valuable opportunities for growth and success. Instead of fixating on an uncertain future, professionals should aim to develop a proactive mindset by setting realistic short-term goals and actively working towards them. This allows individuals to channel their energy into actionable steps rather than fruitless worrying. Embracing uncertainty as a learning opportunity can pave the way for innovation and adaptability in professional endeavors, leading to greater personal satisfaction and career advancement.

Stop Looking for Happiness in Other People

In the realm of professional development, it is crucial to recognize that true happiness and fulfillment do not solely lie in other people. While healthy relationships and interactions undoubtedly contribute to our overall well-being, relying on external sources for happiness can lead to dependency and instability. Instead, it is prudent to cultivate a sense of self-awareness and internal contentment as the foundation of professional success. This involves finding joy in personal accomplishments, setting meaningful goals, and embracing individual passions. By redirecting our focus inward, we can build resilience and develop the emotional intelligence required to navigate the complexities of the workplace.

Consequently, prioritizing self-happiness fosters personal growth and cultivates strong interpersonal skills, enabling professionals to forge genuine connections with colleagues while maintaining a healthy sense of autonomy.

Ultimately, understanding that true happiness emanates from within empowers individuals to take ownership of their own professional journey and create a fulfilling career trajectory independent of others' validation or approval.

Every Setback is a Chance to Learn

When talking about professional development, setbacks are not to be dreaded but rather embraced for their invaluable potential for growth and learning. In fact, every setback provides us with a unique opportunity to reflect upon our actions, identify areas requiring improvement, and recalibrate our strategies accordingly. Instead of succumbing to disappointment or disillusionment, a truly dedicated professional will view setbacks as stepping stones towards success. By dissecting the reasons behind these setbacks, we can uncover valuable insights into our strengths and weaknesses, allowing us to refine our skills and enhance our performance.

Moreover, setbacks offer a chance to develop resilience and perseverance - qualities highly regarded in any professional setting. By harnessing the power of setbacks as catalysts for self-improvement and learning, professionals forge their own path towards continuous growth, proficiency, and ultimate success in their chosen careers.

Here are some survival tips.

- Retrain your brain to react as you do once you have solved the problem, that warm feeling or phew that flows through the body.
- What if everything turns out ok? Just think you have survived every problem that has come your way, so what if you tell yourself what if the worst never happens?
- Train your brain to stop performing continuous worst-case scenario play in your mind.
- Spend your brain power and time working on a solution, stop fearing the worst, and make yourself feel happy.
- Stop hearing your team and start listening to your employees.

Have Fun

In a professional setting, a leader needs to foster a positive and enjoyable work environment. A leader who has fun with his staff creates an atmosphere of camaraderie and teamwork, which boosts morale and productivity. By engaging in a lighthearted manner, such as sharing jokes or organizing team-building activities, the leader can establish a sense of trust and open communication with their employees. This allows for more effective collaboration and the free expression of ideas.

Furthermore, having fun in the workplace encourages creativity, critical thinking skills, and higher job satisfaction among employees. A leader who can balance professionalism and create an enjoyable atmosphere demonstrates strong leadership qualities that inspire employees to perform their best and contribute to the organization's success.

Giving Additional Chances

Providing employees with additional chances is of utmost importance as it promotes a culture of growth and development within an organization. The reality is that mistakes and setbacks are part of any professional journey, and by allowing employees to learn from their errors, we foster resilience and improvement.

Moreover, offering second chances demonstrates empathy and understanding towards individuals facing personal challenges or experiencing temporary lapses in performance. By investing in our employees' growth by providing additional chances, we enhance their skills and cultivate loyalty and commitment. In doing so, we create an environment where employees feel valued, supported, and motivated to strive for continuous excellence. Embracing the notion of second chances acknowledges that people are fallible but capable of redemption, fostering a workplace culture that embraces professional development and promotes long-term success for both individuals and the organization.

Leadership Patients

Being a leader is not an easy feat, and one quality that is indispensable for successful leadership is patience. A leader must possess patience because it allows them to remain composed and level-headed in the face of adversity. Patience helps leaders navigate through tricky situations without becoming overwhelmed or making impulsive decisions. In addition, leaders need patience when dealing with their team members. They must understand that not everyone learns or works at the same pace and be willing to offer guidance and support.

Patience also plays a vital role in building trust and rapport with team members, showing that the leader values their input and respects their growth process. A patient leader listens attentively, fosters open communication, and creates an environment where mistakes are seen as learning opportunities rather than failures. Good things take time, and patient leaders understand the importance of perseverance to achieve long-term success.

Tough Decisions

Leaders must make tough decisions. In the ever-changing and complex business world, leaders frequently face difficult choices that can impact their organization's success. These decisions often involve allocating limited resources, managing conflicting interests, or navigating uncertain environments. Leaders must use analytical reasoning, emotional intelligence, and strong moral character to make these tough calls effectively. They need to gather relevant information, weigh different perspectives, evaluate potential risks and benefits, and determine the best course of action based on their organizational objectives and ethical principles.

Making tough decisions also requires courage, as leaders must take responsibility for the outcomes and be prepared to face criticism or backlash from stakeholders. By embracing this challenging aspect of leadership, professionals can demonstrate their ability to handle adversity and drive their organizations towards growth and resilience.

Don't Worry, Be Happy

Why do we always worry about what we can't change? I can't begin to tell you how much time and stress I've caused myself worrying about what I can't fix. The worst is when a problem arrives Friday evening, and you have the entire weekend to worry. Or late in the evening, and you have all night to worry. I'd have a miserable time because all night or all weekend, I'd play all types of scenarios in my head, including losing my job. I'd go through the three stages of worry:

1. How much money or time will this cost our client?
2. How will this impact my reputation?
3. Will I lose my job?

Painful times, sleepless nights, and some fear thrown in make for a tough mental milkshake.

The incredible thing is it never happened in most cases. It revolved around an apology email or an action plan explaining how to ensure this never happens again. You feel relieved or joyful to have survived that journey and are off to the next. But what if there were ways to skip this whole process?

The Farmer, the Coach, the Teacher

Which one are you striving to become?

Finding your leadership role can be a challenging task, but it starts with self-reflection and understanding your strengths and weaknesses. It is also important to seek out opportunities that allow you to develop your leadership skills, such as volunteering, taking on new responsibilities at your job, or joining professional associations. Building relationships and networking with others in your field can also provide insight into potential leadership roles or mentorship opportunities.

Additionally, attending leadership workshops or seeking professional development training can help you develop the necessary skills and expertise for a leadership position. Remember that being a leader does not necessarily mean having a formal title; it can also involve being a positive influence on those around you through the example you set and the support you provide. Take time to reflect on what kind of leader you want to be and how you can lead by example in your personal and professional life.

The (Coach)

A leader who coaches is a vital asset to any team or organization. This type of leader utilizes their expertise and experience to guide, mentor, and train others to enhance their skills and capabilities. Unlike traditional top-down leadership styles, a coaching leader fosters a collaborative environment where individuals are encouraged to learn from mistakes, take ownership of their work, and push themselves towards growth.

By taking on the role of a coach, these leaders aim to empower their team members through constructive feedback and personalized development plans. They also prioritize ongoing communication with team members to check in on progress regularly and provide support. In doing so, this style of leadership can create a culture that values learning, innovation, accountability, and driving success for the organization.

The (Farmer)

Planting seeds in employees is a vital component of successful organizational management. This involves investing time and effort into developing employees' skills, abilities, and competencies to ensure long-term productivity and success. To plant these seeds effectively, it's crucial to establish clear expectations, provide consistent feedback, recognize strengths and areas for improvement, and offer opportunities for growth and development. Managers must be vigilant in identifying talent within their team to nurture their growth potential continually.

As a result, leaders who commit to planting these seeds can create a thriving environment that fosters creativity, innovation, employee satisfaction, and loyalty and boosts organizational success. Investing in employee development also conveys that the company values its workforce beyond mere labor input but as skilled contributors with the potential for elevated performance output.

The (Teacher)

A leader who teaches is an individual with a profound understanding of their field who takes it upon themselves to share their experiences and knowledge with others. They can effectively communicate complex concepts clearly and concisely, making them easily digestible for their audience. This leader not only imparts practical skills and techniques but also instills a sense of inspiration and motivation in those they teach. Their teaching style is tailored to suit the needs of everyone, allowing for personalized guidance and growth.

Furthermore, this leader provides continuous support and encouragement, empowering their students to take risks, explore new avenues, and develop their own unique perspectives. Through mentorship, feedback sessions, and open discussions, they foster an environment of mutual trust and respect where everyone feels comfortable sharing ideas and seeking knowledge. A leader who teaches uplifts others by equipping them with the tools necessary for success while nurturing their personal growth along the way.

Diplomacy

As a leader, you must simultaneously support company goals and your team's needs. Achieving this balance means maintaining good relations with senior stakeholders and the people you manage through open communication with both parties.

You might also need to use diplomacy when negotiating with outside vendors to ensure your organization comes out well while maintaining a positive relationship with the other company. To be diplomatic, you need to think before you speak, have patience, and show respect to the other people involved.

Example: In many cases, reaching a company goal may mean asking your team to increase their output by working extended hours. In this situation, you may negotiate performance-based bonuses for each team member. This not only helps the company by ensuring your team is motivated to meet their goal, but it also shows your team you value their extra efforts.

Conflict Resolution

Sometimes, conflicts arise between employees or departments, and it is up to those in management positions to ease tensions and unify the workforce. This requires patience, consistent communication, and immediate action.

Quickly addressing any conflicts will ensure a positive work environment for everyone involved. Learning specific de-escalation techniques and conflict management skills can help you navigate these situations. Teaching those skills to your team can help them solve many problems without your involvement.

Example: If two employees have different opinions about the best way to manage a project and begin to divide the team, it's crucial to step in and close the gap. Listening to both sides and mediating a compromise between the employees will help everyone move forward.

Motivation

An effective leader understands the critical role of motivation in driving a team towards success. Motivation is not merely about providing incentives or rewards; it requires a comprehensive approach that considers individual strengths, goals, and aspirations. A skilled leader takes the time to understand their team members' unique talents and empowers them by setting challenging but achievable objectives aligned with their personal growth. The leader builds trust through open communication and actively listens to their team's concerns and ideas, valuing each member's contribution.

Moreover, an influential leader creates a positive work environment by fostering camaraderie, celebrating achievements, and providing constructive feedback. By acknowledging individuals' efforts and offering support when needed, a leader inspires their team members' enthusiasm, commitment, and loyalty. This cultivation of motivation promotes higher productivity levels and fosters a culture of excellence within the organization.

Stress and heavy workloads can affect team morale and threaten productivity. As the leader, you are responsible for monitoring motivation levels and the well-being of your team. To effectively motivate your team, you must set a good example, empower them to achieve personal objectives, and let them work autonomously instead of micromanaging. Take time to learn each employee's ambitions, and then help them gain the skills they need to reach those goals.

Example: If you know an employee is interested in pursuing a senior role, allow them to lead meetings and projects so they can develop their leadership skills.

Decisiveness

Leaders are responsible for making many decisions, often with a quick turnaround time. These range from big decisions, such as hiring a new team member, to small choices, such as selecting a meeting time. The faster and more active you are in your decision-making, the better you will be able to earn your team's trust and confidence.

To improve this skill, it is essential to collect the information you need quickly, weigh potential outcomes, and trust your experience and instincts as your guides. You might also need to admit when you make wrong decisions occasionally.

Example: If you are deciding between two possible candidates for an open position on your team, you'll want to consider their experience and skills, as well as how their personality traits align with the company culture.

Empathy

You may think of empathy as having many emotions or even a weakness. However, empathy can make you a strong leader with employees who respect you and feel appreciated in return. When you are an empathetic leader, you tune into your team's thoughts, feelings and needs and understand how those things might affect their performance.

That does not mean you let your employees get away with things just because they are having a bad day, but you might look for ways to support them when they're going through a difficult time to ensure they can get their work done.

Example: If an employee loses a loved one, you can be an empathetic leader by giving them your sympathies and assuring them they can have the necessary time off work. You might also help get their workload covered while they're gone. Daily empathy might include recognizing the signs of employee burnout and talking to them about it or adjusting their workload.

FAQ that Must Be Answered

Why do you need to improve your leadership skills?

Leaders should always work on improvement, even if they are already successful. All people have room for improvement, regardless of what stage they are in when it comes to their careers. As the leader, you set the tone for your team. As you learn how to be a better leader, you also give your employees the tools they need to succeed in their roles by modeling successful behavior, and it can inspire them to become better leaders as well.

Best Day Ever!

One of the standout days in my professional career was when I successfully closed a deal with a major client that had been in the works for months. The day started out with me feeling confident and prepared after diligently practicing my pitch and reviewing all necessary documentation. As the meeting progressed, I could see that the client was impressed by our proposal and slowly but surely began leaning towards signing on with us. The final moment when they agreed to move forward with our company was euphoric, and it felt like all the hard work and dedication had paid off.

This best day ever came without any worries, as everything fell into place smoothly and seamlessly. It served as a reminder of the satisfaction that comes from achieving goals through perseverance, strategic thinking, and unwavering determination in the face of challenges.

Best Day Ever?

The concept of a "best day ever" can vary depending on one's individual experiences and circumstances. In a professional context, however, the best day ever would involve achieving considerable progress towards an important organizational objective. This could manifest in several ways, such as closing a major business deal, launching a highly anticipated product or service, or successfully completing a demanding project ahead of schedule.

The best day ever might also entail receiving positive feedback from colleagues, partners, or clients that validates one's hard work and dedication to one's craft. While daily obstacles are inevitable in any profession, collaborating with a team of motivated individuals who share your passion for success can make all the difference in experiencing your very best day ever within the workplace.

Worst Day Ever

The concept of a "worse day ever" can have varying degrees of severity depending on the individual and their circumstances. For a professional, this could encompass a range of setbacks that impede progress towards their goals or negatively impact their reputation. It could be losing an important client or deal, experiencing a critical error in a project, receiving negative feedback from higher-ups, or even being let go from a job. The weight of such events can cause significant emotional strain and interfere with productivity, making it even more crucial to maintain composure and find solutions to alleviate the situation. While encountering challenges is an inevitable part of any career path, it is how one responds to and learns from adversity that shapes one's success in the long term.

Employees Are Human

Despite the rapid technological advancements and rise of automation in the workforce, it is important to acknowledge that employees will always be human. Human elements such as emotions, creativity, critical thinking, and communication skills cannot be replicated by machines. Organizations must recognize and value these unique human attributes to foster an inclusive work environment where employees are supported to reach their full potential. Embracing employee diversity, promoting work-life balance, offering training programs for professional development, and encouraging open communication channels can enhance employee engagement and job satisfaction.

As technology rapidly evolves, organizations must invest in their people by providing them with the necessary resources and tools to stay relevant and competitive in today's global marketplace while promoting a culture of mutual respect, trust, and inclusion.

Self-Destruction

Self-destruction refers to the conscious or subconscious act of causing harm or ruin to oneself, often resulting from negative thoughts, behaviors, or decisions. In a professional context, self-destruction can manifest in several ways that severely affect an individual's career and personal growth. It may involve engaging in self-sabotaging behaviors such as chronic procrastination, negative self-talk, sabotaging relationships with colleagues or superiors, or engaging in unethical practices. The primary driver behind this behavior could be deep-rooted insecurities, fear of failure, or mental health issues left unaddressed.

Moreover, self-destructive tendencies hinder professional development by impeding productivity and success while amplifying stress levels. To counteract self-destruction in a professional setting, individuals must seek therapy or counseling if needed, develop emotional intelligence and resilience skills to cope with setbacks effectively, and foster a positive work environment that encourages open dialogue and support among colleagues.

Scared Leadership

Leading with fear is a counterproductive and unethical approach that should be avoided in any professional setting. This outdated management style often leads to a toxic work environment, stifles creativity, and hinders employee motivation and productivity. Instead of empowering and inspiring employees to perform their best, managing with fear instills feelings of anxiety, low self-esteem, and job dissatisfaction. A leader who resorts to fear as a means of control is unable to build trust or establish open lines of communication with their team members.

In contrast, effective managers focus on creating a positive work culture built on trust, mutual respect, and employee engagement. By fostering an atmosphere where ideas can be freely exchanged, and mistakes are welcomed as learning opportunities, managers can inspire their team members to reach their full potential and ensure the long-term success of both individuals and the organization.

The Arrogant Leader

Arrogant leadership in a professional setting can have detrimental effects on both employee morale and productivity. When managers display arrogance, they often dismiss the opinions and ideas of their team members, creating an atmosphere where open communication and collaboration are stifled. This not only leads to decreased employee engagement but also hampers innovation and creative problem-solving within the organization.

Furthermore, arrogant managers tend to take credit for successes while shifting blame onto their employees for failures, fostering a toxic work culture built on fear and mistrust. This type of management style inhibits growth and development among team members, as it discourages them from taking risks or seeking feedback. Organizations with arrogant managers risk losing talented employees who seek workplaces that value their contributions and foster an inclusive environment. Therefore, leaders must adopt humble and empathetic approaches to management that empower their teams instead of undermining them.

Why Can't They Get Along?

There are several underlying factors contributing to employees not getting along within a professional setting.

Firstly, varying personality types and work styles can lead to clashes and misunderstandings. For instance, introverted individuals might prefer working independently, while extroverts thrive in collaborative environments. Secondly, competition among colleagues for promotions or recognition can create a sense of animosity and resentment towards one another. The desire to outshine others often hampers teamwork and fosters an individualistic mindset.

Moreover, ineffective communication or poor management can exacerbate conflicts between employees. Misinterpretation of directives or lack of clarity regarding roles and responsibilities can breed frustration and tension within the team.

Additionally, cultural differences, diverse beliefs, and values may contribute to misunderstandings or biases that disrupt harmonious interactions among coworkers. These factors highlight the importance of cultivating a positive work environment that emphasizes empathy, effective communication, and conflict-resolution strategies to foster better employee relationships for enhanced productivity and overall organizational success.

Listen to Both Sides

One of the fundamental principles in maintaining professionalism and integrity is the commitment to always listen to both sides during any discussion, conflict, or decision-making process. As professionals, it is our duty to gather as much information as possible before forming an opinion or reaching a conclusion. By actively listening to diverse perspectives, we can comprehensively understand the matter at hand, anticipate potential consequences, and foster an inclusive environment that values different viewpoints. This approach not only allows us to make informed decisions and formulate well-rounded arguments but also promotes fairness, respect for diversity, and open dialogue.

Additionally, by listening attentively to both sides, we demonstrate empathy towards others' experiences while minimizing biases that may influence our judgment.

Overall, maintaining this practice of balanced listening ensures professionalism and enhances our ability to navigate complex situations with integrity and impartiality.

Yelling at Your Staff

Yelling at staff members is highly detrimental to maintaining a professional and harmonious work environment.

Firstly, it undermines their motivation and confidence. Employees become demoralised instead of feeling supported and valued, affecting their performance and productivity. Yelling also erodes trust between managers and their subordinates, making it less likely that individuals will approach their superiors with concerns or ideas. This lack of open communication obstructs problem-solving processes and hinders the growth of the business.

Additionally, yelling creates a hostile atmosphere that spreads negativity among the team, increasing turnover rates as employees seek healthier work environments elsewhere. Effective management involves providing constructive feedback calmly and respectfully, allowing for open dialogue that encourages mutual respect and cooperation. By avoiding yelling at staff members, managers can foster an atmosphere of professionalism, collaboration, and dedication necessary for long-term success.

Remain Cool

You know what they say: keeping your cool is the name of the game when it comes to leadership. As experienced leaders know, getting angry in front of staff is a big no-no. But why is that? Well, let's dive into it.

Firstly, losing control and letting that anger show might undermine your authority and credibility as a leader. Your team needs someone who can remain calm under pressure, not someone who becomes extremely angry at the slightest annoyance.

Additionally, displaying anger can create an uncomfortable and unwelcoming work environment for your staff. They might be hesitant to approach you with concerns or questions if they fear setting off another explosive episode.

Lastly, leading by example is crucial in any leadership role. If you want your team to manage their emotions well and keep professionalism intact, then you need to do the same. So, remember to stay calm and collected, and always lead with composure!

Stay Calm

Maintaining composure is a fundamental skill in any professional setting, as it allows individuals to stay focused and exhibit self-control even in challenging situations.

Firstly, it is essential to practice emotional intelligence by recognizing and understanding one's own emotions. This self-awareness enables professionals to respond rather than react impulsively, allowing for more thoughtful and constructive interactions.

Additionally, deep breathing exercises can be an effective technique for regaining composure. By taking slow, deliberate breaths, professionals can activate their parasympathetic nervous system, reducing stress levels and promoting calmness.

Furthermore, developing active listening skills helps professionals empathize with others and gain a better understanding of the situation at hand before formulating a response.

Moreover, seeking support from mentors or trusted colleagues can provide invaluable insights and guidance during stressful moments.

Lastly, engaging in activities outside of work, such as exercise or hobbies, promotes overall well-being, which contributes to maintaining composure when faced with adversity in the workplace.

How Do Leaders Maintain Their Composure?

Being a leader not only requires intelligence and decision-making skills but also the ability to maintain composure in challenging situations. One way a leader can accomplish this is by staying calm and composed under pressure despite any chaos or uncertainty surrounding them. This can be achieved through various strategies such as taking deep breaths, practicing mindfulness or meditation, and reminding oneself of the bigger picture.

Additionally, seeking support from trusted colleagues or friends who can provide an objective perspective can help alleviate stress and keep emotions in check. Leaders must have strong self-awareness, recognize their triggers, and find ways to manage them. This could involve temporarily stepping away from the situation to gather thoughts or considering different alternatives before responding. A leader maintains composure by controlling their emotions effectively, staying focused on goals, and being adaptable to inspire confidence among their team members.

Fear vs Respect

Fear and respect are contrasting emotions that can influence relationships, particularly in a professional setting. While fear may elicit compliance by intimidation or threats, it breeds a toxic environment where creativity and innovation are stifled. On the other hand, respect fosters an atmosphere based on trust, collaboration, and mutual understanding. When individuals feel respected by their colleagues or superiors, they are more likely to be engaged, motivated, and committed to their work. Respect empowers employees to voice their opinions and take risks without fear of retribution or humiliation. It also promotes open communication channels necessary for effective teamwork and problem-solving.

Ultimately, creating an environment that values respect over fear is morally sound and beneficial for organizational success as it nurtures a healthy workplace culture that encourages individual growth and productivity while fostering strong interpersonal connections.

Never Let Your Staff Know What You're Thinking

Sometimes, it might be best to keep your thoughts to yourself when it comes to managing your staff. Transparency and open communication are important in building a healthy work environment. Still, there can be hidden benefits in not letting your employees know what is going on inside your head all the time. Maintaining a certain level of privacy can prevent unnecessary panic or anxiety among your team members. Sharing every single detail about your thoughts and decision-making process might create confusion or even stir up unnecessary drama. It is like that adage says, "Sometimes less is more." Instead of giving away all the practical details, focus on providing clear guidelines, constructive feedback, and support when needed. This way, you will strike a balance between transparency and keeping a sense of mystery. This approach can prove surprisingly effective in building trust and fostering productivity within your team.

They Think I Am Clueless

Do not sweat it if your staff thinks you are clueless sometimes. It happens to the best of us! In fact, being seen as clueless by your team can work in your favor. It shows that you trust and empower them to take charge and make decisions independently. It demonstrates a level of humility and openness to innovative ideas, fostering a healthy work environment where everyone feels heard and valued. Plus, acknowledging that you do not have all the answers encourages your employees to step up and bring their expertise to the table.

Remember, leadership is not about having all the solutions but about creating an atmosphere where collective intelligence thrives. So, embrace the cluelessness every now and then – it might just be the catalyst for great breakthroughs within your team!

Never Let on to Knowing What Your Staff is Up to

It is important to never let your staff know that you are on to them. I mean, come on, everyone wants to feel like they have a little bit of freedom at work, right? Micromanaging and constantly watching over their shoulders can create a tense environment and negatively impact morale. Instead, it's better to establish an open and trusting relationship with your team. Allow them the space they need to be productive and creative without feeling like they are constantly being monitored.

Of course, this does not mean you should turn a blind eye to any issues or shortcomings; it simply means giving them the benefit of the doubt until proven otherwise. Doing so builds a foundation of trust and respect that can strengthen your team dynamics and boost overall performance in the long run.

Employees

Motivating Staff

Motivating staff in the workplace is a critical aspect of effective leadership. It is essential to communicate expectations and goals, ensuring each employee understands their role and responsibilities within the organization.

Additionally, creating a positive work environment can significantly impact motivation levels. This can be achieved by recognizing and appreciating employees' efforts through regular feedback, rewards, and acknowledgement of achievements. Investing in professional development opportunities for staff members can also foster motivation, as it demonstrates a commitment to their growth and advancement.

Furthermore, effective communication channels should encourage open dialogue, allowing employees to voice their concerns or suggestions. Providing autonomy and empowerment fosters a sense of ownership over one's work and increases motivation levels.

Lastly, leading by example inspires staff members as leaders who exhibit passion, dedication, and professionalism to become role models for their team members. By implementing these strategies consistently, maintaining high staff motivation becomes an attainable goal in any professional environment.

Employee of the Month

So, do you know that iconic "Employee of the Month" award that many workplaces have? Well, let us spill the tea on it. It is a way for companies to recognize and appreciate their stellar employees each month. It is like their moment in the spotlight, where they strut their stuff and get some extra bragging rights around the water cooler. Usually, they get a shiny plaque or certificate to proudly display on their desk. But here is the thing: it is not just about superficial recognition.

Being named "Employee of the Month" often comes with additional rewards like special parking spots, gift cards, or even an extra vacation day. Although some may scoff at this whole endeavor as just a silly popularity contest, it can boost morale and motivation among coworkers. Plus, it allows management to acknowledge outstanding performance and inspire others to step up their game, too.

Overall, Employee of the Month is a fun little tradition that adds a dash of lighthearted competition to any workplace while recognizing hardworking individuals who truly deserve it!

How to be the Best Employee

To become the best employee, it is crucial to consistently display a strong work ethic, exceptional skills, and unwavering dedication to your job.

Firstly, diligently prioritize tasks, setting realistic goals and deadlines that align with organizational objectives. Continuously seek avenues for personal growth and development by staying abreast of industry trends and acquiring relevant certifications.

Moreover, effective communication is vital for building relationships within the workplace. Listen to colleagues and supervisors while concisely articulating your thoughts to enable efficient collaboration. Demonstrating adaptability and flexibility during challenging situations will foster the resilience necessary for progressing in one's career.

Additionally, displaying professionalism by adhering to ethical standards and maintaining utmost integrity establishes trust amongst peers and superiors alike. And always approach criticism constructively as opportunities for improvement can be invaluable in honing skills further.

Ultimately, excelling as an employee requires constant self-evaluation, perseverance, and a commitment to delivering high-quality results in all facets of one's professional life.

Leader, not Parent

Hey, so I have come to realize that being a leader doesn't mean you have to parent everyone around you. It is easy to fall into the trap of wanting to control and dictate every move of your team or group, but that's just not how effective leadership works. People are adults, capable of making their own decisions and learning from their mistakes. As a leader, it is our job to provide guidance and support, and set clear expectations, but we cannot coddle them like a parent. Instead, let's foster an environment where individuals feel empowered to take ownership of their work and make independent choices. Give them space to grow and learn from their experiences. Trust me, this approach not only builds self-sufficiency in your team members but also allows for greater collaboration and innovation.

So, remember, you are a leader, not their parent – embrace it!

Why do I Owe You?

Well, let me break it down for you in a casual way. When you run a business, your staff plays a crucial role in its success. They are like the fuel that keeps the engine running smoothly. So naturally, as an employer, you owe them respect and gratitude for their efforts.

But it goes beyond simply basic decency. Your staff deserves to feel valued because they contribute to achieving your company's goals day in and day out. They give their time and expertise, often going beyond their job descriptions to ensure customers are satisfied and targets are met.

And let us not forget about their dedication – the countless hours they put in to make things happen behind the scenes. Mutual trust and appreciation form the foundation of any successful team, so if you want to retain talented employees who genuinely care about your business, owing them acknowledgment and rewards is non-negotiable.

Know Your Staff

A good leader utterly understands the importance of knowing their staff on a personal level. It goes beyond just memorizing names and job titles; it is about understanding each employee's strengths, weaknesses, and motivations. When leaders know their staff well, they can tailor their management approach to suit everyone, ensuring everyone feels valued and supported in their roles. They can identify opportunities for growth and development, placing employees in positions where they can excel and thrive.

Additionally, knowing one's staff fosters a sense of trust and loyalty within the team. Employees feel more comfortable approaching their leader with concerns or ideas because they feel seen and understood. Leaders who take the time to get to know their staff build more cohesive teams and create an environment where everyone can reach their full potential.

Who's Right?

To effectively lead a diverse group of individuals, it is paramount for a leader to cultivate the art of listening to each side. This means they must not only hear what each team member has to say, but also genuinely understand and consider their perspectives. By actively listening, leaders demonstrate respect for others' opinions and foster an environment where every voice feels valued. Such inclusivity encourages open dialogue, creativity, and innovation among team members, leading to more well-rounded decision-making.

Moreover, by carefully considering multiple viewpoints before making a final call, leaders can avoid any unintentional biases or blind spots that may hinder progress or cause unnecessary conflicts. Therefore, to truly connect with their team and harness the full potential of diversity within it, a leader must embrace the value of listening wholeheartedly and strive to understand all sides involved.

Ranking Employees

To effectively rate each employee, it is paramount to establish clear and measurable criteria that align with the individual's job responsibilities, competencies, and objectives. This can be achieved through a combination of quantitative data, such as sales figures or project completion rates, and qualitative assessments derived from ongoing performance evaluations and observations. A fair rating system should consider not only an employee's outcomes but also their behaviors and attitudes towards work. Regular communication with employees throughout the evaluation period provides an opportunity to address any concerns, offer constructive feedback, and set goals for improvement.

Furthermore, it is imperative for managers to remain unbiased by considering both strengths and weaknesses objectively without favoritism or prejudice.

Ultimately, assessing employees' contributions holistically enables fair, transparent, and accurate ratings that encourage professional growth.

Special Needs or Accessible Employees

Leading special needs employees requires a thoughtful and inclusive approach. One key aspect is fostering open communication and understanding between the employees and their colleagues. This means constantly encouraging team members to ask questions, seek clarification, and share their experiences in a casual and non-judgmental manner.

Moreover, it's crucial to provide reasonable accommodations that meet their specific needs while maintaining the integrity of the job tasks. It may involve flexible schedules or adjusting workplace conditions, such as providing noise-canceling headphones for individuals with sensory sensitivities.

Additionally, promoting a culture of empathy and respect creates an environment where everyone feels valued and supported. This can be achieved by offering disability awareness trainings, ensuring supervisors model inclusivity, and implementing performance evaluations that consider individual strengths rather than solely focusing on weaknesses. By creating an atmosphere that appreciates diversity, managers can effectively manage employees' unique needs in a casual yet compassionate way.

Amazing Employees

"I am always astounded at the level of dedication and challenging work you put into every situation. Thank you for all the hours you worked over the weekend and yesterday to ensure our client's needs were successfully met."

As a manager, it is important to keep a certain level of staffing to ensure that operational goals are met and business goals achieved. I have decided that our current workload requires adding two more employees. This will help us effectively manage our projects and respond to our client's needs more efficiently and accurately. The hiring process will be conducted using a comprehensive selection criterion to find qualified and competent candidates who fit into our company culture while also meeting the requirements of the role we need them for.

Additionally, newly hired employees must receive thorough training and integration into our existing team so they can effectively contribute towards achieving overall success for our organization.

Disagreeable Employees

Disagreeable employees can be a real thorn in the side of any business. They come in all shapes and sizes, from those lacking motivation and enthusiasm to those actively undermining the company's goals and morale. In a casual workplace, disagreeable employees can be particularly difficult to lead as they may not take their responsibilities as seriously as they would in a more traditional setting.

Unfortunately, dealing with these individuals can be an ongoing challenge for management or HR teams. While addressing such behavior quickly and constructively is a must, the best strategy is often prevention through effective recruitment processes that identify the right fit for the company culture and values. Maintaining open communication channels with staff members also helps nurture a positive work environment where everyone feels valued and supported.

Ultimately, recognizing and addressing bad employee behavior is critical to ensuring productivity, job satisfaction, and long-term business success.

Troubled Employees

Managing a problem employee can be challenging, but it is possible to turn things around with the right approach. Open and honest communication is critical. Schedule a one-on-one meeting with the employee to discuss the issues at hand and listen to their perspective without judgment. This will help build trust and understanding between both parties. Provide clear expectations, guidelines for improvement, and specific examples of behavior that needs to change. Offer support by providing necessary training or resources to help the employee improve their skills. It is also essential to address any underlying issues contributing to their performance problems, such as personal challenges or job dissatisfaction. Regular feedback sessions should be scheduled to track progress and provide constructive criticism when needed. If all efforts fail, termination may become necessary. Still, it should be approached as a last resort after exhausting all other options for improvement. Always include your Human Resources partners.

Leaders Do Not Argue with Employees

When it comes to being a leader, there is often the misconception that arguing with employees is an effective way to assert dominance or maintain control. However, true leaders understand that arguing only breeds negativity and hinders productivity within the team. Instead of arguing, leaders prioritize effective communication and seek to understand their employees' perspectives. They recognize that disagreement does not equate to incompetence but rather represents an opportunity for growth and innovative thinking. Leaders foster a culture of open dialogue where individuals feel comfortable expressing their opinions without fear of retribution. By setting this tone, leaders encourage collaboration and create an environment where everyone's contributions are valued, enhancing critical thinking skills and increasing employee morale. Leaders who refrain from arguing with their employees cultivate trust, mutual respect, and shared success.

Leaders Remember Names

In the realm of professional leadership, a key trait that distinguishes exceptional leaders is their ability to remember and address employees by their names. This simple gesture holds significant importance as it fosters trust, empathy, and a sense of belonging within the workplace. By making a conscious effort to recall and use employees' names consistently, leaders show that they value individual contributions and recognize them as unique individuals rather than mere cogs in the organizational machinery. Such personalized attention creates a positive work environment where staff members feel seen, respected, and appreciated for their efforts.

Furthermore, remembering employee names helps leaders build stronger relationships with their team members, allowing for open communication channels and more effective collaboration. It demonstrates an investment in each person's personal growth and development while enhancing overall team morale and motivation. This diligence exemplifies professionalism at its core and sets the foundation for strong leadership that inspires loyalty and fosters productivity.

Worrying About Employees' Past

When considering an employee's past, employers need to approach the matter with a professional and fair mindset. While it is natural to have concerns about a candidate's previous employment history, focusing solely on their past may not reflect their potential for success in the current role. It is crucial to remember that people can grow and change over time, so assessing candidates based on their present skills, qualifications, and references should be prioritized instead. Engaging in thoughtful interviews and reference checks will provide more insight into a candidate's ability to perform well in the desired position.

Furthermore, it is essential to ensure that any inquiries about an employee's past are conducted within legal boundaries and do not discriminate against certain protected characteristics such as race, gender, or religion. By taking a balanced approach and evaluating candidates based on their current abilities rather than dwelling on their past, employers can make informed decisions that lead to successful hires while adhering to ethical practices.

Giving Additional Chances

Providing employees with additional chances is of utmost importance as it promotes a culture of growth and development within an organization. The reality is that mistakes and setbacks are part of any professional journey, and by giving employees the opportunity to gain experience from their errors, we foster resilience and improvement.

Moreover, offering second chances demonstrates empathy and understanding towards individuals facing personal challenges or experiencing temporary lapses in performance. By investing in our employees' growth through providing additional chances, we not only enhance their skills but also cultivate loyalty and commitment. In doing so, we create an environment where employees feel valued, supported, and motivated to strive for continuous excellence. Embracing the notion of second chances acknowledges that people are fallible but capable of redemption, fostering a workplace culture that embraces professional development and fosters long-term success for both individuals and the organization.

Inspirations

Mentors

Having mentors is crucial for personal and professional growth. A leader can benefit immensely from the wisdom and guidance imparted by experienced mentors who have traversed similar paths. Mentors serve as a source of inspiration, offering advice based on their own successes and failures. They provide invaluable insight into the challenges and complexities of leadership, helping leaders navigate uncharted territories with confidence and resilience.

Furthermore, mentors act as sounding boards for ideas and offer constructive feedback, allowing leaders to refine their strategies or approaches. The role of a mentor extends beyond simply sharing knowledge; they instill ethical values, encourage self-reflection, and challenge leaders to push their limits. This support system establishes a solid foundation for continuous learning and development, enabling leaders to make informed decisions while fostering their own potential.

Ultimately, having mentors empowers leaders to excel in their roles by blending experience with innovation to drive organizational success.

Finding a Real Leader to Follow

Finding real-life leaders can be an immensely valuable experience for anyone aspiring to become an effective leader. While theories and academic studies play a crucial role in understanding leadership principles, observing and learning from experienced leaders in action provides practical insights that no textbook can offer. Real-life leaders can translate theoretical concepts into tangible actions, enabling followers to witness firsthand the application of leadership skills in various contexts. By studying their behaviors, communication styles, decision-making processes, and problem-solving techniques, one can gain invaluable knowledge and develop a deep understanding of what leading truly means.

Additionally, interacting with real-life leaders allows individuals to ask questions, seek guidance, and receive personalized advice tailored to their unique situations. These interactions enable aspiring leaders to acquire wisdom rooted in experience while building a network of mentors who can support their growth.

Ultimately, learning from real-life leaders ensures a well-rounded development that combines both theory and practice for effective leadership in the professional world. Some of my favorites are on the following pages.

Julius Caesar

Caesar was a great leader for a multitude of reasons.

Firstly, his ability to inspire and unify people was unparalleled. His charismatic personality and powerful presence commanded respect and loyalty from his followers.

Additionally, Caesar possessed exceptional strategic thinking skills, which enabled him to make calculated decisions and lead successful military campaigns. He prioritized the well-being of his troops, ensuring they were adequately trained and equipped, which fostered a strong sense of camaraderie amongst them.

Furthermore, Caesar was an excellent communicator; he had the remarkable ability to connect with people from all walks of life, allowing him to galvanize support for his cause. He showed compassion towards those he ruled over, implementing impactful reforms that improved the lives of many Romans.

Lastly, Caesar's unwavering determination and courage in the face of adversity solidified his position as one of history's greatest leaders.

Joe Gibbs

Joe Gibbs was an exceptional leader who left a profound impact on the world of American football. His greatness stemmed from his ability to motivate and inspire his players, as well as his exceptional coaching skills. Gibbs created an environment of trust where every player felt valued and supported. He possessed a remarkable talent for identifying the strengths of each individual and strategically incorporating them into a cohesive team.

Additionally, Gibbs' meticulous diligence and ability to adapt to changing circumstances set him apart as a leader. He excelled in studying game footage, formulating innovative strategies, and making split-second decisions that transformed the outcome of games.

Moreover, Gibbs' relentless commitment to excellence pushed his teams beyond their limits. It instilled in them an unwavering determination to succeed. His tremendous success with the Washington Football Team, including three Super Bowl victories, cemented his status as one of the most outstanding leaders in football history.

Martin Luther King

Martin Luther King Jr. was a great leader because of his unwavering commitment to justice, equality, and nonviolent activism in the civil rights movement. His charismatic personality and powerful oratory skills allowed him to effectively communicate his message of hope and equality to millions of people, inspiring them to join the struggle for racial justice. He had an unobstructed vision for a more inclusive and equal society, which he tirelessly fought for until his untimely death. King's ability to rally people from diverse backgrounds and build coalitions demonstrated his strong leadership skills.

Moreover, his strategic use of nonviolent resistance to challenge systemic racism earned him international recognition. By employing peaceful tactics like sit-ins, protests, and boycotts, King highlighted the brutal reality of racial injustice while advocating for change without perpetuating violence. Martin Luther King Jr.'s legacy continues to inspire leaders around the world who aim to confront discrimination and build an inclusive society for all.

Steve Jobs

Steve Jobs was a visionary leader and a remarkable mentor who deeply impacted the lives of those who had the privilege to work closely with him. His mentoring style was unique and effective, driven by his relentless pursuit of excellence and passion for innovation. As a mentor, Jobs placed great emphasis on pushing his mentees beyond their comfort zones and encouraging them to think differently. He demanded nothing less than perfection from his team members, challenging them to constantly surpass their own expectations.

Yet, beneath the tough exterior, Jobs also provided guidance and support, always ready to share his insights and wisdom. He invested time in developing personal connections with each mentee, inspiring loyalty through his integrity and charisma. Jobs pushed individuals to discover their true potential, molding them into creative problem solvers and critical thinkers. His mentorship transformed careers not only by imparting technical skills but also by instilling a relentless drive for success that would continue long after his influence ended.

Tony Robbins

Tony Robbins, an internationally acclaimed motivational speaker and life coach, stands as a prominent figure in personal development. With four decades of experience, Robbins has become renowned for his ability to mentor individuals from all social classes and guide them towards achieving their fullest potential. His dynamic and captivating speaking style resonates deeply with audiences around the globe, motivating countless individuals to act and transform their lives. Utilizing a unique blend of psychology, neuro-linguistic programming techniques, and practical strategies, Robbins empowers his mentees to overcome limiting beliefs, discover their true passions, set clear goals, and develop effective habits.

Moreover, his unwavering focus on fostering personal relationships ensures he establishes strong connections with those he mentors. By imparting invaluable wisdom and insight through various platforms such as seminars, books, audio programs, and one-on-one coaching sessions, Tony Robbins continues to inspire professionals across industries to reach unprecedented heights both personally and professionally.

Family & Friends

My Wife

My wife is not just my partner in life; she is also a remarkable business friend and leader. Her natural ability to connect with people and build strong relationships has proven invaluable in her professional endeavors. Whether negotiating deals or leading teams, she has a genuine charisma that inspires others to follow her lead. She understands the importance of empathy and actively listens to individuals' concerns, creating an environment where everyone feels heard and valued. I have witnessed her navigate tough business decisions with grace and poise, weighing both the financial implications and the impact on people's lives. She genuinely cares about the well-being of others, ensuring that success is achieved collectively rather than at the expense of individuals. Her tireless work ethic and her innate talent for problem-solving allow her to tackle challenges head-on whilst finding innovative solutions.

My wife is not only an exceptional leader but also a trusted confidante whom colleagues seek advice from time and again. Through her leadership skills, compassion, and unwavering dedication, she continues to excel as both a business friend and an influential leader in various aspects of life.

My Daughter

My daughter is authentic when it comes to customer service. I mean, this young lady lives and breathes it! And here is why: she genuinely cares about people and their satisfaction. She has this innate ability to put herself in the customers' shoes and anticipate their needs before they even voice them. It's like she has some kind of mind-reading superpower! Not only that, but she always goes the extra mile to ensure every interaction is a positive one. Whether it is a smile, a friendly greeting, or even a small gesture of kindness, she understands these little things can brighten someone's day and create lasting impressions. It is not just about meeting expectations for her; it is about exceeding them and leaving people with an unforgettable experience. That is why she stands out from the crowd and has earned the reputation of being the point of reference for exceptional customer service. I am so proud of her and proud to call her my daughter.

My daughter is also a real people leader! From an early age, she had an innate confidence and charisma that drew others to her like moths to a flame. Witnessing how effortlessly she can command attention and guide groups towards achieving common goals is incredible. Whether on the soccer field or in a school project, she has this uncanny ability to unite people with her infectious enthusiasm and unwavering determination. She knows how to bring out the best in everyone around her, effortlessly empowering and motivating them to reach for the stars. It is not just about being in charge; she genuinely cares for those under her watch and ensures their voices are heard.

While others may strive for popularity, my daughter strives for inclusivity and making everyone feel valued. Her natural leadership qualities will undoubtedly take her far in life as she continues positively shaping the world around her one person at a time.

My Parents

Looking back, I realize that my parents were indeed my first leaders. Growing up in a close-knit family, they served as guiding lights, shaping and molding me into the person I am today. Their actions and principles taught me valuable life lessons that extend far beyond what any textbook could offer. They led by example, demonstrating integrity, resilience, and compassion in every aspect of their lives. Their unwavering support and encouragement provided a safe space for me to explore my passions and take risks. Whether it was teaching me the value of hard work or instilling empathy towards others, their influence was profound. They may not have held prestigious titles or commanded large teams, but their leadership skills were unmatched in the way they nurtured and guided me through life's difficulties.

As I walk through my own journey now, I can't help but be grateful for their love and guidance, which set a strong foundation for me to become a confident leader myself.

Mister X

I've had my fair share of bosses throughout my career, ranging from amazing to not-so-amazing. One leader who truly stood out to me, and I will call him Mr. X, is my former manager – a director at an outsourcing firm. He had this incredible ability to bring out the best in his team while maintaining a laid-back and approachable demeanor. Mr. X believed in empowering his employees rather than micromanaging them. Mr. X never hesitated to listen to our ideas or provide guidance whenever we needed it. His transparent communication style created an environment where everyone felt comfortable sharing their thoughts and concerns openly. Mr. X's leadership style fostered a keen sense of camaraderie within our team, ultimately leading to increased productivity and success.

Working with someone like Mr. X taught me the importance of trust, respect, and collaboration in a professional setting without sacrificing that laid-back vibe we all crave in the workplace.

Pastor Hall

My Pastor's ability to teach the word and impart knowledge of scripture is truly remarkable. With a deep understanding of theology and years of experience, he has honed his skills in delivering sermons that are not only engaging but also informative and thought-provoking. Pastor Hall's passion for studying the Bible shines through in every message, as he carefully dissects passages and provides historical context to help our congregation better grasp the meaning behind the text. Through his eloquent delivery and insightful teachings, Pastor Hall can connect with individuals on a spiritual level and inspire them to live according to biblical principles. His dedication to spreading God's word and commitment to helping others grow in their faith and making him a highly respected and effective leader within our church community.

Furthermore, Pastor Hall's inclusivity is remarkable and inspiring, as he ensures that all members feel welcomed and valued within the Church community. This exceptional display of leadership, combined with an unwavering sense of compassion, creates an environment that encourages personal growth and transforms lives for the better

Those Amazing Ladies

I would like to express my sincere gratitude and appreciation to all the strong and positive women who have emerged as influential leaders in various fields. Your remarkable efforts, relentless dedication, and exceptional skills have not only broken barriers but also paved the way for progress and equality. As pioneers of change, you have overcome countless hurdles, shattered glass ceilings, and pushed boundaries to define a new era of leadership. Through your unwavering determination and commitment to your goals, you inspire countless others while challenging societal norms that limit gender-based opportunities. Your aptitude for collaboration, strategic thinking, empathy, and resilience highlights the qualities essential to successful leadership. Thank you for inspiring generations to come and empowering women worldwide to aspire for greatness and seize their potential in every professional realm possible.

Past and Present Leaders I've Worked For and With

I can't even begin to express how much I've grown and learned by working with leaders throughout my career. These folks have been like guiding lights, showing me the ropes and teaching me invaluable skills that no textbook or classroom could ever provide. From the moment I stepped foot into the professional world, I had the privilege of observing their strategies, decision-making processes, and problem-solving abilities firsthand. They've instilled in me a sense of discipline, determination, and confidence that has helped shape my leadership style and allowed me to thrive in challenging situations. Their wisdom has taught me the importance of effective communication, fostering teamwork, adapting to change, and never shying away from taking calculated risks. Working with these exceptional individuals has made me realize that true leadership isn't about flashy titles; it's about being humble yet assertive and inspiring others through actions rather than words alone. I owe so much of my success to these leaders who have become mentors and inspirations—forever grateful for their impact on my life both professionally and personally.

Me

As a humble leader with a heart and vision for the lives of those I lead, I prioritize building strong relationships and fostering an inclusive work environment. I believe in leading by example and creating opportunities for growth and development within my team. By being humble, I actively seek feedback from others, recognizing that I do not have all the answers and can always learn from different perspectives. This humility allows me to connect on a deeper level with my team members, understand their aspirations, and support them in achieving their goals.

Additionally, having a clear vision enables me to set strategic objectives that align with our collective purpose, ensuring everyone is working towards a common goal. With compassion as the driving force behind my leadership approach, I strive to empower my team members to unleash their full potential while fostering a culture of respect, collaboration, and continuous improvement.

The Army

So, let me tell you about my teenage experience in the army. It was a unique and transformative period in my life. At first, I was not sure what to expect as a teenager entering such a disciplined environment. But boy, did it shape me! From grueling physical training to developing mental toughness, I learned the true meaning of resilience. The friendships I formed during those years were forged through shared challenges and triumphs—those are bonds that will last a lifetime. Serving alongside individuals from diverse backgrounds taught me invaluable lessons about teamwork and empathy. Balancing the rigors of military life with the typical teenage ups and downs was no easy feat.

In the end, though, it taught me discipline, time management, and adaptability like nothing else could have. Looking back now, I realize how much those experiences molded me into the person I am today—someone who can face adversity head-on with confidence and determination.

Epilogue

Key Points to Keep in Mind Regarding Leadership

We've covered a lot of ground, but I thought it would be great just to provide a little reminder of what we've covered.

Being a successful leader requires a particular set of skills and qualities. A leader should possess the ability to motivate and inspire their team and guide them towards success. There are a few fundamental rules of leadership that can help any leader achieve success in their role.

Firstly, a leader should always strive to be a role model. This means displaying the same qualities that they would expect from their team. They should also be open to feedback from their team and be willing to learn from mistakes.

Secondly, a leader should always be prepared to take responsibility for their team's successes and failures. This is an important trait, showing the team that the leader is committed to their development.

Thirdly, a leader should ensure that their team is well-informed. This means providing them with the necessary information and resources to help them achieve their goals.

Fourthly, a leader should make sure their team is well-motivated. Motivation is critical to success, and a leader should be able to provide it. They should also be able to recognize when their team needs extra support.

Finally, a leader should be able to communicate effectively. Good communication skills are vital in any team environment, and a leader should be able to clearly convey their ideas and instructions.

These are the top rules of leadership that any leader should strive to follow. By following these rules, a leader can ensure their team is well-motivated, well-informed, and successful.

I Love Leadership

I absolutely adore being a leader, and let me tell you why!

First off, there is something truly empowering about guiding a group of individuals towards achieving a common goal. It allows me to utilize my communication, problem-solving, and decision-making skills to positively influence the team's progress. Being a leader also provides the opportunity for personal growth. From learning how to effectively delegate tasks to understanding different personality types and identifying what motivates everyone, I am constantly developing valuable skills that extend beyond the realm of leadership.

Another aspect I love is the sense of fulfillment that comes from seeing my team members thrive and succeed under my guidance. Witnessing their growth and achievements brings an indescribable joy that makes it all worthwhile.

Overall, being a leader both challenges and rewards me in ways that few other roles can match, making it an incredibly fulfilling experience!

Nobody is Coming. Be Your Own Hero!

In the professional realm, it is imperative to possess a mindset of self-reliance and taking initiative. The notion that no one will come to your rescue fosters a sense of personal responsibility, empowering individuals to overcome challenges and strive for greatness. Waiting for external forces to intervene not only hinders progress but also undermines one's ability to grow and develop professionally. Embracing the spirit of being their own hero allows professionals to tap into their potential, harnessing their skills and knowledge to navigate through obstacles. Rather than passively waiting for opportunities or succumbing to setbacks, professionals need to cultivate resilience, proactively seeking solutions and forging their own path towards success.

Embodying this philosophy fosters a proactive approach towards professional growth while fostering an independent mindset crucial in today's competitive landscape.

Made in the USA
Columbia, SC
08 November 2024